UHTRED'S FEAST

BERNARD CORNWELL was born in London, raised in Essex and worked for the BBC for eleven years before meeting Judy, his American wife. Denied an American work permit, he wrote a novel instead and has been writing ever since. He and Judy divide their time between Cape Cod and Charleston, South Carolina.

SUZANNE POLLAK, born in Beirut now living in Charleston, South Carolina, is the co-author of a number of cookery and entertainment books including *The Pat Conroy Cookbook* and *Entertaining for Dummies*. She is currently the Development Director of the annual Charleston Literary Festival. It was at this that she met Bernard Cornwell and the idea for this book was born.

Bernard Cornwell

with Suzanne Pollak

Uhtred's Feast

Inside the world of
THE LAST KINGDOM

HarperCollins*Publishers*

When using kitchen appliances please always follow the manufacturer's instructions. If cooking with an open flame or unconventional oven, please observe caution and seek professional guidance where applicable.

HarperCollins*Publishers*
1 London Bridge Street
London SE1 9GF

www.harpercollins.co.uk

HarperCollins*Publishers*
Macken House, 39/40 Mayor Street Upper
Dublin 1, D01C9W8, Ireland

Published by HarperCollins*Publishers* 2023

1

Introductions and stories © Bernard Cornwell 2023
Recipes © Suzanne Pollak 2023

Illustration on p. 1 © Alla Pashkova/Arcangel Images
Illustrations on p. 21, p. 95, p. 191 © Bridgeman Art Library

Bernard Cornwell with Suzanne Pollak asserts the moral right to be identified as the authors of this work

A catalogue record for this book is available from the British Library

HB ISBN: 978-0-00-835292-9
TPB ISBN: 978-0-00-853225-3

The short stories in this book are entirely works of fiction. The names, characters and incidents portrayed in it, while at times based on historical figures, are the work of the author's imagination.

Printed and bound in the UK using 100% renewable electricity by CPI Group (UK) Ltd

MIX
Paper | Supporting responsible forestry
FSC™ C007454

This book is produced from independently certified FSC™ paper to ensure responsible forest management.
For more information visit: www.harpercollins.co.uk/green

UHTRED'S FEAST

is dedicated to

Jordan Enzor

whose extraordinary knowledge helped
so much with this book.

Our thanks.

Contents

THE MAKING OF ENGLAND

I was raised on the coast of Essex, a place of marshes, tidal creeks and rivers. From the roof of our house I could see the Thames widening into its huge estuary and could watch ships pushing upriver towards Tilbury or the London docks. Sailing ships were common; mostly Thames barges with their huge gaff-rigged russet mainsails carrying agricultural produce to the city, but I also remember being bewitched by the sight of a tall ship, all sails set, making that voyage.

What I was seeing was an echo of history. The Thames, of course, had long been a major waterway into England. Square-sailed Roman ships slid in and out of the Thames, while much later some of our most famous warships like HMS *Victory* were built on its banks and sailed to triumph on the world's oceans.

As a child, however, I was more interested in other ships that had haunted the estuary, ships that had engendered terror; the longships of the folk we call the Vikings. I remember when I was six years old how Prince Georg of the Danish royal house visited the nearby village of Ashingdon and presented to the villagers a Danish flag and a fine model of a Viking longship (which still hangs in the Parish Church of St Andrew). The reason for this generosity was to commemorate the battle of Assandun between King Cnut of Denmark

3

and King Edmund Ironside of England. The Danes won, and Cnut subsequently became King of England. As a child I was fiercely interested in history, and the longship hanging in St Andrew's nave fired my imagination and curiosity.

A decade or so later I discovered the Anglo-Saxon poem, the 'The Battle of Maldon', which was a description of a battle between Byrhtnoth, leader of an army of East Saxons, and a Viking band that had taken up residence on Northey Island in the River Blackwater, which is not that far from Ashingdon. The Vikings won (again), but I recall a teacher telling us that the poem was 'fanciful' because the East Saxons on the bank of the river could never have heard a challenge shouted from Northey Island; it was too far. That drove me and a few friends to Maldon where we proved such a challenge was indeed audible, that expedition being the only serious original research I have ever undertaken.

My childhood had thus given me an abiding interest in the Anglo-Saxon period, but I soon came to realise I was woefully ignorant about it. Some time between the Romans abandoning Britain and the arrival of the Normans, a whole country had been created, England, and despite a more than adequate education I had no idea how that had happened. I also realised I was not alone; that an English school curriculum suggested that English history began in 1066. It is almost as if there is no history for England before the arrival of William the Conqueror, except for the primary school stories of Alfred burning the cakes and King Cnut failing to turn back the tide.

In 1939 a song became immensely popular, recorded by, among others, Dame Vera Lynn; 'There'll always be an England' was the song, and it implied there always had been an England, yet in 1939 England was only a shade over 1,000 years old. The creation of England happened during that

4

pre-1066 history. Unfortunately we can't give an exact date to that momentous event, but at some time in the autumn of 937 the Anglo-Saxon army led by King Æthelstan destroyed a combined army of Vikings and Scots at a place called Brunanburh. Brunanburh was a major battle in England's history and for years after was simply called 'the great battle', it even inspired the *Anglo-Saxon Chronicle* to break into verse:

Never was there more slaughter
On this island, never as many
Folk felled before this,
By the sword's edge – as books and aged sages
Confirm – since Angles and Saxons sailed here
From the east, sought the Britons over the wide seas,
Those proud warsmiths. They overcame the Welsh,
Glory-hungry earls, and took hold of this land.

It might have been the great battle, but it was swiftly forgotten and even the place where the battle had been fought was also forgotten. We now know the battle was fought on the Wirral, and while it is tempting to say that the conflict was the birth moment of England, it is more accurate to see it as a part of the process. That had begun much earlier, when Æthelstan's grandfather, King Alfred, had the ambition to unite the different Anglo-Saxon kingdoms.

By Alfred's time there were four kingdoms, Wessex in the south, East Anglia to the east, Mercia in the midlands, and Northumbria stretching to the Scottish border. Two of those kingdoms, East Anglia and Northumbria, were under Danish rule, Mercia was under constant pressure from the Danes, and only Wessex was apparently safe under Saxon governance. That changed in 878 when the Danish Vikings invaded

Wessex and drove Alfred to the Somerset marshes where he became a fugitive. Somehow he raised an army and inflicted a devastating defeat on his enemies at Ethandun, and in the subsequent years, and under his son, King Edward, Mercia became a part of Wessex, and the Saxons then inflicted defeats on the Danes in East Anglia. Alfred's ambition had been to unite all those lands where English, the language of the Saxons and Angles, was spoken. It would not just be language that united the peoples, but religion too. The Danes and other Northmen who held so much land in Britain, were pagans, and Alfred was determined that they should become Christian.

The victory at Brunanburh weakened the Northmen's hold on Northumbria and that kingdom swiftly became a part of what was now to be called Englaland. There were to be other fights to seal the conquest, but by the time the Normans (descended from Vikings as their name implies) invaded Englaland, they discovered a united country with a working system of government, taxation and law. That law was policed by shire-reeves, from which comes our word 'sheriff'. The shires were Saxon inventions, but under the Normans the more usual word 'counties' was used, and the sheriffs were consigned to America's wild west.

There was an irony in the story of the Saxon conquest of England. The struggle against the Northmen was almost a repetition of an earlier invasion when the Saxons had first come to Britain. That happened as the Romans were abandoning the island, leaving behind them a string of forts along the eastern seaboard designed to repel the Saxon incomers. Those forts failed, and a succession of Angle and Saxon invaders landed, pushing the native Britons outwards into what is now southern Scotland, into Wales, Cornwall, and south across the sea to Brittany. There is an echo of that brutal merciless time in the *Anglo-Saxon Chronicle*'s report on Brunanburh, claiming that the famous battle marked the greatest slaughter

> . . . since Angles and Saxons sailed here
> From the east, sought the Britons over the wide seas,
> Those proud warsmiths. They overcame the Welsh,
> Glory-hungry earls, and took hold of this land.

That poem, written in 937, also contains an echo of tribal triumph over an ancient enemy and a celebration of the defeat of a new enemy who had first been recorded in the *Anglo-Saxon Chronicle* in the year 787. In that year three ships arrived on the coast of Wessex;

> Then the reeve rode there and wanted to compel them to go to the king's town because he did not know what they were, and then they killed him. These were the first ships of the Danish men which sought out the land of the English race.

Those three ships might have been the first, but they were not the last. More and more raiders harried the British coast. The most shocking of these raids occurred in 793, when the Northmen sacked the monasteries on Lindisfarne and at Jarrow. The ransacking and murders at Lindisfarne (clearly visible from the ramparts of Bebbanburg) appalled Saxons:

> This year came the dreadful forewarnings over the land of Northumbria, terrifying the people most woefully. These were immense sheets of light rushing through the air, and whirlwinds and fiery dragons flying across the firmament. These tremendous tokens were soon followed by a great famine: and

not long after, on the sixth day before the ides of January in the same year, the harrowing inroads of heathen men made lamentable havoc in the Church of God on Holy Island, by rapine and slaughter.

But these attacks were still raids; the Northmen came, they burned, stole, killed and enslaved, then left, yet that all changed in 865 when a large army of Vikings sailed from Ireland to England and, instead of raiding and leaving, they stayed. They were led by Ivarr Ragnarson, usually known by the name Ivar the Boneless, the son of Ragnar Lodbrok who had been killed by the King of Northumbria in 865. It seemed Ivarr wanted revenge because he led his army into Northumbria and captured that kingdom. Now the threat was not just coastal raids, but the existence of Danish kings and warlords who had settled. The Danes controlled most of northern and eastern England and wanted it all. By 876 the *Chronicle* reports that the invaders had 'shared out the lands of Northumbria and were engaged in ploughing and making a living for themselves.' Raiders don't plough land unless they expect to be there to reap the harvest. The raiders had become settlers, and if the Saxons were to take back their land they had to defeat the settlers.

In 878, before the battle of Ethandun, it must have seemed that the Saxons had been overcome and the proud warsmiths were the Danes, and the fate of the Saxons would be to follow the Britons into exile. Alfred defied that fate by defeating the Great Army at Ethandun and so preserving his kingdom of Wessex, and it was from Wessex that the crusade to unite the Saxon kingdoms into one country began.

And it was a crusade. The Saxon invaders had occupied a land where Christianity had been introduced by the Romans, and the new owners of that land were pagans, preferring the old northern gods like Odin and Thor. It was not until the seventh century that a missionary effort initiated by Pope Gregory I succeeded in converting the pagan Anglo-Saxons to Christianity. That conversion was not instant, but the 'new' religion gradually replaced the old pagan creed, with North-umbria the last of the four kingdoms to institute Christianity as the official religion. An optimist might have thought that wor-shipping the Prince of Peace would end the violence between the Saxon kingdoms, and between those kingdoms and the neighbouring Scots and Welsh, but the spoils of war were more attractive than the rewards of peace, while the neces-sity of spreading the gospel meant that warfare against pagans was regarded as virtuous. Alfred was intent on regaining as much Saxon land as possible, but alongside that ambition was another; to convert the pagans. The struggle to unite England was as much religious as territorial.

At the heart of the struggle was the attraction of England; not the concept of a nation, but the nature of the territory that would eventually belong to the English. On the whole the Northmen came from lands that did not offer wide pasture-land and rich crops; Britain did. This was a period when men and women had to live off the land, and the more fertile the land, the better the living, and England, like Ireland, had vast amounts of good farmland. This was the prize that the Saxons had won from the Britons, and were now losing to the Vikings. And, just as the Saxons had taken over working farmsteads, so now did the Vikings; they were capturing and exploiting an existing economy; a rich agricultural economy.

The conquered Saxons, like the defeated Britons before them, undoubtedly resented their new rulers, but life would not have changed much, a life dictated by the seasons and the need to tend crops and livestock. For a Saxon farm labourer it probably made no difference that he was ditching for a Viking instead of a Saxon, at least not until his daughter married one of the Viking's followers and his grandchildren grew up speaking a melange of both languages. They did not expect *eyren* for breakfast, but asked for *eggs* instead, and as those children grew, they assimilated more and more Viking words into the English language. In *The Stories of English* David Crystal lists two dozen words that have survived from their Norse origin into today's English: anger, awkward, bond, cake, crooked, dirt, dregs, egg, fog, freckle, get, kid, leg, lurk, meek, muggy, neck, seem, sister, skill, skirt, smile, Thursday, window.

That is a brief list, there are many many more words in modern English that were introduced by the Scandinavians, like *they*, *their* and *them*. In short, despite the warfare and religious enmity, the invaders were being assimilated. They did more than contribute words and DNA to their new land, they changed its names too. If you live in the north or east of England in a place whose name ends in *by*, *toft* or *thorpe*, then almost certainly you live on land once possessed by the Vikings. I grew up in an Essex village called Thundersley, which stood on a prominent ridge overlooking the Thames Estuary. The name appears to mean 'Thunor's ridge', Thunor being the god Thor. It was probably a Saxon name, commemorating their old allegiance to Thor, but there were certainly Viking settlements nearby, and local lore insisted that the Bread and Cheese Hill, which led to the ridge's summit, was named for the battle cry of Saxons wielding their 'broad and sharp' swords as they charged the Vikings. I have long wanted to believe that, but am yet to be convinced.

I was fortunate to grow up in a place that was layered with

history, even if I did not entirely understand how tangled those layers were, but fate could have landed me on the Northumbrian coast where, in the middle of the sixth century, an Angle warlord named Ida the Flamebearer led his warriors ashore and captured a wooden fortress built atop a massive volcanic rock. His grandson hugely expanded the lands controlled by the fortress, and on his death left it to his wife, Bebba, and so it became known as Bebbanburg; Bebba's fortress. Bebbanburg still exists, only today it is called Bamburgh Castle and is built of stone instead of the wooden walls that Ida conquered and inhabited.

None of this would have meant anything to a small boy living on Thor's Ridge in the county named for the East Saxons far to Bebbanburg's south, but in middle age I discovered my natural father who was living in British Columbia, and he had a family tree stretching all the way back to Ida the Flamebearer and beyond to Odin himself. By that time I had decided I wanted to write a series of novels that would more or less tell the tale of England's creation and, delving into my family tree, I discovered some ancestors named Uhtred who had lived through that period. At birth I was given my mother's surname, but my father, who never married her, was called Oughtred – the link was obvious, and I decided to tell the story of England's birth through a character named Uhtred.

Uhtred is fictional, and if I have played merry hell with his real history it is because first I feel I have a descendant's right to do that, and second very little is known of the real men named Uhtred who lived over a thousand years ago. I have almost certainly done them an injustice in suggesting that my Uhtred was a pagan, but that loyalty to the old Saxon religion makes his dealings with the extremely pious King Alfred more interesting. Not that his life away from negotiating Alfred's piety is uninteresting, because he lives through the tortuous and frequently brutal events that create England.

It was not an easy birth. To make Alfred's ambition real, the rulers of Wessex had to overcome the nationalist prejudices of the East Anglians, Mercians and Northumbrians, and all four kingdoms had a history of warfare with each other. They were rivals, and the rivalry often descended into bloodshed. Other kings had wanted to unite Saxon England, the most famous of them Offa of Mercia, who ruled not only Mercia, but Kent and parts of East Anglia. Some documents style Offa as Rex Anglorum, King of the English, but the title flatters him as he never controlled all of what became England. He was undoubtedly a successful warrior king, but the title King of the English describes an aspiration rather than an achievement.

The cause of English unification was helped by the irruption of a new enemy. 'From the fury of the Northmen,' an Irish monk wrote, 'good Lord deliver us.' The Northmen were the Vikings, Scandinavian adventurers who, equipped with brilliantly designed ships and savage weapons, sailed from their homelands to steal treasures from the rest of Europe; those treasures were gold and silver, usually found in one building conveniently marked with a cross, and anything else that could be sold; including humans. There were thriving slave markets for the sale of captives, and the advent of slavery in Britain long predates the Vikings.

To stand beside a river like the Blackwater in Essex is to understand the terror of the Vikings; to imagine their dragon-beaked ships slowly coming upriver through a misty dawn, and the rowers' benches filled with hardened warriors who will come ashore with axe, spear and sword to take whatever they wish; your livestock, your harvest, your belongings, your wife, your children, and your life. The Vikings were an existentialist threat to the Saxons, just as the Saxons had been to the Britons, and the Vikings seemed unstoppable. They had soon settled most of Northumbria, had captured East Anglia, and were making massive inroads into Mercia, and it was the sheer danger of their ultimate victory that forced Wessex and Mercia to forget old enmities and forge an alliance to resist the invaders. For a time they tried bribery, paying the Danes to keep the peace, but those payments of Danegeld simply sharpened Viking hunger; the only solution was war. In 878 it seemed that the Danes had won that war when they successfully invaded Wessex, so driving Alfred into refuge in the Somerset marshes. That was the low point of Anglo-Saxon fortunes, but miraculously Alfred managed to assemble an army and defeat the Danes at Ethandun. For the remainder of his reign, and through the reign of his son, Edward, the West Saxon led army pushed the Danes back.

The strategy for that successful resistance against an enemy that for too long had appeared invincible was Alfred's. He built burhs throughout Wessex and Mercia. A burh was simply a fortified town, ringed by a wall. The wall was a high earthen bank topped by a timber palisade. The earth banks at Wallingford in Oxfordshire and at Wareham in Dorset are still visible, and evidence of the enormous manpower needed to make such structures. Within the burh's defences was a town or large village that would provide protection for local inhabitants fleeing a Viking raid. Towns such as Chester, Bridgnorth, Tamworth, Stafford, Hertford, and Warwick were all burhs, some, such as Chester, using the Roman walls as their defences. London was a burh, as was Winchester, Alfred's capital city. Much of the wealth that attracted Vikings was protected inside the burhs, and Alfred drew up strict regulations as to how they were to be defended. Local men, drawn from the surrounding farms, were required to man the walls with a density of around four men per pole. A pole was roughly sixteen feet.

The strategy worked. The Vikings were free to roam the countryside, but most of what they wanted to capture was behind high walls and, though the Vikings were fearsome warriors, they lacked the skills of siegecraft. If they did settle down to starve a burh into surrender they made themselves a target for the Saxon army. Alfred's son Edward and his daughter Æthelflæd continued the strategy, building burhs further north into Mercia and so driving the Viking settlers ever northwards.

In 937 Anlaf Guthfrithson, the Viking King of Dublin, was eager to claim his ancestral right to the throne of Northumbria. He made an alliance with King Constantine II, King of Scotland, and Owain, King of Strathclyde. Strathclyde was essentially a Welsh kingdom in southern Scotland, a place where the Britons displaced by the Saxons had fled for refuge. Both Owain and Constantine feared the growing power of Wessex and joined Anlaf in what was designed to be a massive invasion of the English-speaking territory. The troops from Scotland marched south on the west coast and joined Anlaf's forces that had crossed the Irish Sea to the Wirral, where they were met by Alfred's grandson, Æthelstan, who led the army of Wessex reinforced by Mercian troops. So happened the battle of Brunanburh, which the *Chronicle*'s poet would describe as 'no greater slaughter'. Much of that slaughter occurred when the Hibernian-Vikings and the Scots fled the battlefield in defeat and were ruthlessly massacred by the pursuing Saxons. The historian Michael Livingston, in his impressive book *The Battle of Brunanburh*, writes of the battle that the importance of Brunanburh 'lies not in the land gains under Æthelstan that were solidified – if transiently so – on that battlefield. To the contrary, Brunanburh was remembered as a rousing call for a nation. What Æthelstan won in 937 was more than a kingdom of soil, it was a kingdom of the heart and mind: those who followed him to the throne ruled not as kings of Wessex, but as kings of Britain. Alfred the Great might have dreamed of a national entity we might call "England", but the battle had made it real.'

The creation of England was a long and brutal process. The Angles and Saxons began arriving in Britain some time either in the fourth century or the early fifth, and it would take half a millennium for them to seize the land that became England and form it into one nation. It would take 150 years between the first Viking attacks and the slaughter on the Wirral to repel the Northmen's assault on that nascent nation. It is a tale of almost constant warfare, stretching across the whole island of Britain. Farnham, in Surrey, is a beautiful small town with elegant Georgian streets, art galleries and historic buildings. It is quintessentially English, comfortable and prosperous, yet in 892 it was the scene of a fierce battle between a large Viking army and the forces of Wessex led by Alfred's son, Edward. It somehow seems incongruous to imagine a blood-soaked battle in gentle Farnham, yet it happened, and there were many other such battles in the creation of England, and those battles were ghastly affairs.

There were few missile weapons. Spears could be thrown and arrows loosed, but the bows used were hunting bows, not the lethal longbow of later wars, and the arrows could be stopped by a good willow shield, or by a mail coat reinforced with a thick leather lining. The real fighting was done at close quarters by men hardened by experience. A great warlord like Uhtred of Bebbanburg would lead his own warriors, all of them armoured and equipped with the best shields and weapons, and also a force of men from his lands who might not have mail or even an iron helmet, but would dress in leather or a padded jerkin and wield weapons from their rural life; foresters' axes, sickles, fish-spears, or even clubs.

The real fight would be between the trained warriors, and it was fought at a brutally close distance. The poetry of the Anglo-Saxons tells of the shield walls, which would clash and so begin the butchery. The most prized weapon was a warrior's sword, which might have a blade almost three feet long made of carbon-hardened iron – steel. In the stifling close work of clashing shield walls it was cumbersome and could only be used as a stabbing weapon, for which the seax was better designed. The seax, and some authorities believe the weapon gave its name to the Saxons, was a short-sword, not dissimilar to the Roman gladius, and when several ranks of men are heaving against an enemy and are thus crushed together at the point of contact, the shorter sword is easier to wield. Other men carried axes, using the blade's beard to haul down an enemy's shield and so open him to a lunge from a sword, seax or spear.

To break an enemy's shield wall, as evidently happened at Brunanburh, was to shatter his ranks and cause panic, and fleeing men are easier to cut down. After Æthelstan's men split the enemy shield wall at Brunanburh the victorious Saxons 'pursued the hated peoples (for) the length of the day. (They) hewed the fugitive harshly from behind with mill-sharpened swords.' The poet in the *Anglo-Saxon Chronicle* clearly relishes the slaughter and also offers a picture of men sharpening their blades on the revolving stone of a watermill.

The country Æthelstan claimed had been dreamed of by his

grandfather, Alfred, whose ambition had been to unite those folk who spoke the English language. If the nadir of Saxon fortunes was in 878, when Alfred had been forced to flee into the Somerset marshes as his enemies occupied his kingdom, then the revenge was sealed fifty-nine years later at Brunanburh, and Britain at last had a Saxon kingdom united by language, custom and religion. Englaland was born.

Yet Englaland was not wholly English. Daniel Defoe describes it best in his poem 'The True-Born Englishman':

> Thus from a Mixture of all Kinds began,
> That Het'rogeneous *Thing, An Englishman*:
> In eager Rapes, and furious Lust begot,
> Betwixt a Painted *Britain* and a *Scot*.
> Whose gend'ring Offspring quickly learn'd to Bow,
> And yoke their Heifers to the *Roman* Plough:
> From whence a Mongrel halfBred Race there came,
> With neither Name, nor Nation, Speech or Fame.
> In whose hot Veins new Mixtures quickly ran,
> Infus'd betwixt a *Saxon* and a *Dane*.
> While their Rank Daughters, to their Parents just,
> Receiv'd all nations with promiscuous lust.
> This Nauseous Brood directly did contain
> The well-extracted Blood of *Englishmen*.

The infusion of Saxon and Dane was enthusiastically happening in northern and eastern England where intermarriage was common and to this day many a true-born Englishman or woman has Scandinavian DNA. My Uhtred, I call him mine to separate him from my Uhtred ancestors, illustrates this assimilation. He marries Gisela, a Dane, and their children would have grown up speaking and mingling both languages.

His tenants include both Angles and Danes, and both fight in his war-band. He clings to the religion of the Danes, worshipping Odin, Thor and a score of other deities, not because they are Danish, but because they are the same gods of the ancient Saxon religion, and also because such loyalty to a pagan creed annoys Alfred and his entourage of prattling priests.

It was the threat of Scandinavian dominance that drew the Anglo-Saxon kingdoms together to resist the invaders. There were huge battles, massacres and cruelty, though out of that horror emerged what we would call a multi-cultural society. And throughout that mayhem the huge fortress of Bebbanburg remained in Saxon hands, and that puzzled me. How had my ancestors kept their home when they were surrounded by Danish territory? I suspect the answer was collaboration, but I preferred a more noble solution and so devised the fictional exploits of Uhtred. His tale might be fictional, yet behind the adventures I imposed on Uhtred are real events, those long-ago and mostly forgotten battles that forged a country. Fictional history is not real history, novelists leave that to real historians, but our books must be authentic, and authenticity is in the mundane details: What did they wear? How did they travel? What did they eat?

When it came to Uhtred's diet I could safely assume he had cattle, sheep, goats, pigs and deer as sources of meat, and there would have been wheat, barley (for bread and malt for brewing), rye, beans and peas. He lived by the sea, so would have enjoyed fish and eels, and sometimes seal or whale meat. I knew that Uhtred, being an aristocrat and a warlord, would have a privileged diet, which meant he ate far more meat than less fortunate folk and once in a while would even taste imported wine. His meals, in the books, mainly consist of bread, cheese, ale and salted meats. This scanty menu attracted the attention of Suzanne Pollak, a close friend and noted food writer. She wanted to fill the gaps in my 'menu', and so began researching Saxon and Viking food, and even cooked some for me (though, on my insistence, kept carrots from the ingredients). Her research led to this book, and I am hugely grateful to her and to Jordan Enzor, whose knowledge of ancient food is encyclopaedic.

King Alfred did not live to see his dream of a united Christian England come true. But through his vision, his stubborn opposition to the Northmen, and his careful governance, his successors did see England born. And when, in 1066, an invasion led by the grandson of a Viking, William I, conquered England, they took over a country with an established society, a legal system, and a language that survived the Norman storm. That storm did not mark the beginning of England's history but interrupted it. Alfred, whatever Uhtred thinks of him, surely deserves to be called 'the Great'.

Part One

HOME

Historical Background

During the Anglo-Saxon period, in what we now call Britain, most people lived in rural areas or in villages with easy access to food sources. It was a time when much of England was still forested, but where the land was cleared, the soil – particularly that close to the rivers – was rich and fertile, and so this was where settlements sprang up and, with them, pockets of cultivated land. The growth of enclosed land, of borders, fences, walls or hedging, would happen later, with the arrival of the Normans, so at this time, farmland was more open and more freely available to ordinary people. In many cases, they would use this land to provide food not only for themselves, but also for the local lord, as payment of their 'food rent' – essentially a tax that took the form of goods rather than money. The abundance of easily farmed land for the cultivation of crops was one of the attractions for incoming Northmen, many of whom decided to settle.

Keeping animals was key to the sustenance of most households. The cheapest and easiest animals for smallholders to rear domestically were pigs, as they could be kept fairly close to home and released to forage in the local woods. In some hillier areas, people also kept a few sheep – though these were often reared for their wool rather than their meat – while most households kept chickens, as well as geese and ducks if there was water nearby, both for their meat and eggs.

Cows, which needed rich and extensive pastureland, were prized both for their milk and their meat, but were mostly kept by the lords and their tenant farmers rather than individual smallholders. However, beef was not as highly valued as it is today – milk products were the more important, and cattle were essential to producing these. The very word for 'riches' or 'money' in Old Norse, *fé*, has a root meaning of 'cattle', so for each cow that the farmer could not successfully support over the winter, they sustained an economic loss. Having to slaughter a cow to eat for its meat was in some ways an admission of failure, not success.

Indeed, farmers had to make a careful assessment of their hay and grain supplies, and decide how many animals could be overwintered, with the strongest and most productive being retained and the others slaughtered for meat. As slaughtering was mainly done at the end of the grazing season (slaughtering time for cattle and sheep was in October, pigs in November to December), meat was very much a seasonal product.

The lords and their followers, of course, were able to hunt, which gave them meat from wild boar and goats, hares and rabbits (which were both very popular and could be found in the nearby land). Falconry also provided wild birds for the table, along with other small game, although larger ones were usually guarded by the landowners. Venison (deer) was likely only in the banqueting hall, and not in your average homestead.

Growing your own was also standard practice for the Anglo-Saxons. In villagers' gardens and in the land around settlements, more root vegetables were grown than green: no potatoes yet, but carrots, turnips, onions, cabbages, leeks, fennel, peas, fava beans and beetroot. Orchards provided apples and pears, and wherever there was space, in the yard or in nearby land, beehives would be built. Honey was essential for making mead, but it was also the only sweetener available. It was such a desirable product that it was regularly used as a form of payment. Ale was similarly prized, as it was a safer, tastier and therefore preferred alternative to water.

Bread and rolls, however, were perhaps the most central part of Anglo-Saxon living. The common term for bread at this time was *hlaf* (loaf), and its importance in people's diet is evidenced by what they called their lords (*hlafward* or 'loaf guardian') and ladies (*hlaefdige* or 'loaf kneader').

Bread would be made from rye and barley, and sometimes also wheat. In the earlier times it would be baked indoors at home on flat skillets, or in outside stone ovens built over a fire. Later, however, there were communal ovens in mills, controlled by the local lord. As there was little use for coins, payment for this service was taken as a percentage of the wheat, barley or rye.

Professional bakers were around from 2000 BC or earlier, but bread-making was a common domestic skill. Leavened (risen) bread was made in a number of ways, primarily with wild yeasts that simply float in the air. Leaven (the rising agent) is believed to have been discovered in Egypt by accident – wild yeasts probably found their way into a batch of old dough, supposedly 'spoiling' it, and when it was baked anyway, the happy result was a lighter bread with an excellent flavour. The next discovery was to keep part of the dough back to flavour and leaven the next day's bread.

An alternative method was to make bread with dried yeast

produced from the fermenting liquor of brewing beer – a process that dates from well before the Anglo-Saxon period. The word for dry yeast comes from *doerst*, the dregs of beer, referring to the yeasty sediment that was slow-acting and resulted in a heavy sour bread. The yeast was washed in fresh water and spread out to dry on a board, then cut up and stored. This dried yeast could be kept for several months and, when needed, a piece was broken off and crumbled into warm water.

We know that Anglo-Saxons formed their loaves into small and large sizes. In Edward the Elder's will, for example, he refers to 200 large and 100 small loaves. Paintings also show us that loaves were round and about the same size as our loaves are today.

Other forms of cooking were done over an open fire, inside the dwelling in the centre of the living space (which was usually a single room) for most of the year. Meat could be roasted, resting on stones beside the fire or sometimes in free-standing covered ovens outside, or it could be put on a spit hanging over the fire, which would be turned by a handle, occasionally by a useful small child. For anything not roasted or baked, a cauldron would be hanging over the fire – stewed meat, for example. Anglo-Saxons would have washed beef, say, in water, soaked it for possibly 12 to 48 hours, and then boiled it. Stewing for a long time made tough meat palatable and kept in the nutrients. Any leftovers or foraged greens could be added to the pot.

Eating itself would demarcate the waking hours. The Anglo-Saxons would sit down for just two meals a day: one at daybreak before starting the daily chores, and another at the end of the day, which meant quite early in winter times. Platters were often wooden, and most people ate with their fingers, unless dining in the great hall. Occasionally, in return for services, villagers might dine at the local lord's table, and for this people brought their own knives.

Recipes

The recipes in this book represent the taste and spirit of the food of the time, using the same animals, raised and wild, the same plants, raised and wild, and the same preservation techniques.

The Anglo-Saxons – and the Vikings – cultivated, raised, hunted or fished the raw materials and made the ale and the wine themselves. This approach is inspiring to many of us cooking today, even in very different circumstances.

Note that all the recipes are suitable for 4 people, unless stated otherwise.

Note on Fat

Fats are crucial for cooking and contain important nutrients. The Anglo-Saxons would have had butter in the months when cattle, goats and sheep were able to eat grass, but in the colder months, milk production would have stalled and, although butter was sometimes preserved in bogs over the winter, they would have relied on animal fats instead.

If you are uncomfortable creating your own animal fats, feel free to use butter. Pastured fats are best, as they are higher in omega-3, far lower in omega-6, and also contain the best nutrients. Use the best-quality fats you can.

Vegetable oils were unheard of. Olive oil would have been available via trade, which waned at times, but it was expensive and had a tendency to rancidity. If you prefer using olive oil, please do, but know you will be eating as only the Anglo-Saxon nobility could afford.

Recipes

MEAT

Pork Belly ✛ Cracklings ✛ Pork Chops with
Apples ✛ Roasted Leg of Pork ✛ Salt Pork ✛ Salted and
Smoked Pork Leg (Ham) ✛ Smoked Pig's Head
✛ Caraway Roasted Ribs

GARDEN

A Spring Pottage ✛ Ale-glazed Carrots
✛ Parsnip Chips ✛ Cabbage, various ways
✛ Turnips, various ways ✛ Saxon Compote

DAIRY AND BAKERY

Egg Cake ✛ Frittata with Beef Crisps
✛ Bread ✛ Unleavened Oatcakes
✛ Barley Flatbread ✛ King Alfred's Cakes

MEAT

Pork Belly

A wonderful meat, with additional benefits that come from salting before smoking, which preserves the meat but doesn't require such large amounts of salt (a very expensive commodity back in Saxon times). Also, preparing bacon allows the preservation of the all-important cooking fats used over winter, as butter was a summer product.

Salting and smoking pork

The process is simple, and you can choose to use sugar (honey for the Saxons) – or just a salt base. The additional flavourings are completely up to you, but two suggestions are provided here.

One includes two variations of salt: table salt and a very commonly available flavouring from ancient times, seaweed or kelp. There is record of seaweed being used to wrap foods for storage as well as flavouring; seaweed and kelp powder can be found in supermarkets that have an 'international section'.

For the other recipe, use salt, honey and roasted dandelion root (from tea bags, unless you choose to go even more historical and dig up your garden's roots for roasting!).

The aforementioned tea bags are found in many modern supermarkets in the tea aisles. In this case, we are just using what was available in Saxon times.

- ❖ **1 pork belly, skin removed (you can ask the butcher to do this or do so at home and reserve it for cracklings [see page 35])**
- ❖ **Your preferred seasoning mix (see intro)**
- ❖ **Smoke woods – cherry, apple and oak are wonderful**

Depending on the size of the pork piece, the amount of seasoning you use will vary. First and foremost, salt it well, rubbing it into all the nooks and crannies of the meat. If you see the salt soaking right in, sprinkle with more. Let the salt set in for a few minutes before adding any honey or your other seasonings. The kelp powder can be added along with the salt, as it is essentially ocean vegetable salt! If using honey, don't baste the meat, but do ensure you cover it well.

Set the seasoned belly atop a wire rack set in a roasting tin, which will allow air to circulate right around the meat. Cover with foil and put this in the fridge to cure and dry for a week.

To smoke, follow the directions for your type of smoker or barbecue setup. You want to focus on smoking the belly while also cooking it. You want the lower smoking temperatures for this, as you do not want to render out the fat, nor cook the meat to tenderisation. Smoke for as long as you like, but close to 6 hours is sufficient.

Cracklings

Skin and fats on meat make for delicious treats. It doesn't always have to come as part of a roast, you can make these over your campfire, hearth fire, or in the oven. These protein and energy bites make wonderful additions to pottages, eggs, soups or can be eaten simply as snacks.

- ❖ **900g (2lb) pork skin with fat, or pork belly with skin, cut into 4cm (1½in) squares or rectangles**
- ❖ **Enough lard to almost cover the cut pieces (or you can use peanut or vegetable oil)**

Preheat the oven to 180°C/350°F/gas 4.

Place the fat and/or skin pieces in a roasting tin and coat with the lard or oil, then place in the oven. Cook for 1 hour, or until the pieces are browned and the skins float, puff and crack.

Remove the pieces with a mesh spoon and transfer to a plate lined with kitchen towel to drain. They might be cooked at this time, but you can cook them again if you want an even lighter texture. Raise the oven temperature to 200°C/400°F/gas 6, allow the oil to heat up in a roasting tin, and return the cracklings to the hot oil in the oven for another 10–12 minutes until crispy. Keep an eye on them to make sure they do not burn. Transfer to a plate lined with kitchen towel to remove any excess fat.

Pork Chops with Apples

Bacon and ham kept all winter long, so pigs would be butchered late in the year. Fruit was often served alongside meats by the Saxons, and apples ripened in the same season, so made a perfect match for pork. This recipe would have been enjoyed right after slaughter by both peasants and nobles.

Adult Saxon pigs weighed 70–80kg (155–175lb) around the year 1000; however, one thousand years later, adult pigs can weigh up to 350kg (770lb). Chops are cut from the loin, which runs from the hip to the shoulder and contains a small strip of meat called the tenderloin. Buy the best pork chops you can find – it is literally impossible to make an inferior pork chop superior.

- ❖ **Olive oil or bacon fat, for frying**
- ❖ **Pork chops – try to get a nice thick slice of fat on the side of the chop**
- ❖ **Fresh sage leaves**
- ❖ **Apples, thickly sliced**

Heat a cast-iron frying pan over high heat. When the surface is hot, spoon or pour a slug of fat into the pan. You are sautéing the chop, so you need a little more fat than a bare sheen – using enough hot oil is how the fat crisps and becomes delicious.

When the oil starts to pop or 'spit', after about 30 seconds, lay the pork chops in the pan and leave to cook for 5 minutes, then turn them over. When you turn the chops, place the sage leaves and apple slices around the meat and cook, turning once, until crispy and brown.

Depending on the chops' thickness and the temperature of the pan surface, the second side should be done in 3–5 minutes. The chop is finished when the second side's fat is crispy but the interior is pale pink. Stick a knife tip into the middle of the meat and take a look at the colour – it's a fine line between pinky perfection and grey overtones. (If you have an instant-read thermometer, it should read 60°C/140°F.)

Roasted Leg of Pork

Envision a feast in the Saxon hall. A fresh leg of pork, as opposed to a salt-cured leg, makes for an enjoyable presentation – get one with the skin on, and ideally still with the foot attached. Then, whether left on or off, the foot can be saved for a wonderful stock thickener (see page 123), or enjoyed at the table by a special guest!

This is a dish imagined at court, so the spices utilised – ground cloves and fennel pollen – would only have been available to those with the means for obtaining them through the network of trade. Fennel produces flowers, like those of a yellow Queen Anne's lace plant, and then seeds. It is very easy to grow, and one flower head produces an abundance of pollen, which you can crumble with your fingers. Anise has a flavour reminiscent of liquorice, which will lead the mind to recall forgotten feasts.

Serves 8
  ❖ **A leg of pork, skin on, foot attached (ideally) – about 3kg (6½lb), bone in**
  ❖ **Salt, for rubbing**
  ❖ **Fennel pollen, for coating**
  ❖ **Freshly ground cloves, for coating**

At least 2 days prior to roasting, prepare the meat. Score first, using a sharp knife (the pig skin can be a challenge with a dull blade) into a diamond pattern, 2.5cm (1in) in diameter. This will represent scale mail when roasted well, and it allows the fat to better render. After scoring, liberally rub the meat with salt. Since this is a big cut of meat, it will take these two days to draw the salt into the centre of the leg.

After salting, sprinkle over enough fennel pollen to just coat, then do the same with the ground cloves (you can use pre-ground cloves, but freshly ground using a mortar and pestle or spice grinder ensures you get a fresher flavour).

After applying the rub, let the leg sit in the fridge, uncovered, for 2 days. This allows the meat to absorb the salt and flavours, and the skin to dry for better crackling when it comes to roasting.

Bring the leg to room temperature before roasting for 2 hours. Preheat the oven to 230°C/450°F/gas 8 (full whack!), then roast the leg for 35–40 minutes, or until you have a nice crackling skin (bubbled up and crisped). Drop the temperature to 160°C/325°F/gas 3, cover the foot with foil, and slow roast for about 3½ hours, or until the meat is tender and pulls apart easily.

Carve as you wish but serving up the sliced ham with the diamonds of crisp pork skin set to the side works well.

Salt Pork

Salting was essential in Anglo-Saxon times; it prevented meat from decaying and spoiling by pulling out the moisture. You can use 'sea salt' here, but it will invariably be a bit more expensive, and all salt deposits are 'sea salts' anyway.

Salted pork has been a flavourful addition to nearly any dish since ancient times. The pork can come from various parts of the pig: trimmings from ribs, a chunk of the belly, cheeks and jowls, or whatever is economical. Keep your trimmings.

- ❖ **Extra pork, with some fat on it**
- ❖ **Salt flakes**

The result you want is pork well surrounded and covered with salt, not sitting in the liquid that can release from the meat. Heavily salt all over the pork, and place it on a drying rack set atop a roasting tin, to allow any excess moisture to draw out and not pool around the meat. Allow the pork to air out and dry for a day – a full planet rotation. This can be done in the fridge, on a table or on a worktop. The salt will protect the meat from any pests, so you really want it completely caked in salt with no gaps.

After it has spent its 24 hours in the air and drying out, the meat is ready for storing. For this, simple plastic containers are great – any bin shape or cylinder. Pour in a good base of salt, and stack in or arrange the pork atop it. If layering, you want enough salt in between the pork trimmings, so they are not touching the other pieces. The same goes when laying them out side by side. Layer and surround, leaving no air gaps, and completely cover with salt.

This keeps indefinitely in the sealed container and does not require refrigeration, since you will cook the end result. Do not ingest raw, though.

When you want to eat it, soak the meat pieces in at least one change of water – any bowl sufficient enough to allow water to submerge the pork will do – to remove some of the salt, then drain. If eating the salt pork as a main dish, soak in two changes of water, or possibly more. Your tastes will affect how you like it. Depending on the number of soaks, keep in mind that the pork will salt the finished dish, so adjust how you season the rest of the ingredients appropriately. When cooking, the meat can be cut into pieces or cubes and fried like bacon.

Salted and Smoked Pork Leg (Ham)

Smoking was another favoured method of the Anglo-Saxons for preserving meat. For best results, use a pork leg with the skin on, because the skin will cause the fat to baste the meat as it smokes and roasts. The skin itself will take on a wonderful texture, too.

Serves 8
- ❖ **1 leg of pork, skin on**
- ❖ **Sea salt, for rubbing**
- ❖ **Good charcoal**
- ❖ **Your preferred smoking wood (apple, cherry, oak, etc. – Saxon or Danish woods)**

Pat the leg of meat dry with kitchen paper, then score the skin with the traditional diamond pattern. Generously coat the outside of the leg with the salt, rubbing it all over. Wrap with cling film and place in the fridge for at least 24 hours, to allow the salt to penetrate the meat.

After this time, prepare your cooking fire. If you are cooking on the barbecue, light a large chimney starter three-quarters filled with charcoal briquettes. When the top coals are partially covered with ash, pour them evenly over half of the barbecue. Allow the coals to heat until almost white. Place some wood chips or chunks on the coals. Set the cooking grate in place, cover the barbecue and open the lid vent completely. Heat until hot and the wood chips are smoking, about 5 minutes. Brush clear and oil the cooking grate, then unwrap the pork leg and place it flat side down on the cooler side of the grill. Cover the grill (position the lid vent directly over the meat if you are using charcoal) and cook for 2 hours.

Before the pork comes off the grill, adjust the oven rack to the middle position and preheat the oven to 150°C/300°F/gas 2. If using a smoker, follow the guidelines on the smoker manual. When the leg is finished on the barbecue or smoker, transfer the pork, flat side down, to a 32 x 23cm (13 x 9in) baking tin. Cover the pan tightly with foil and roast in the oven until a fork inserted into the meat meets little resistance and an instant-read thermometer registers 100°C (210°F) – about 2½ hours.

Remove the pork from the oven, cover it with a tent of foil and let it rest while you crisp the skin. Increase the oven temperature to 200°C/400°F/gas 6 and line a rimmed baking sheet with foil. Using tongs, remove the skin from the pork in one large piece. Place the skin, fatty side down, on the prepared sheet. Transfer to the oven and roast until the skin is dark and crispy and sounds hollow when tapped with a fork, about 25 minutes, rotating the sheet halfway through roasting.

Smoked Pig's Head

There's a lot of meat on a pig's head, and if you have access and the desire to do so, it makes for some excellent hash, as the meat is full of flavour. Smoke the entirety of the head and you can use all of it, but leave out the brains. The tongue is pure pork flavour – just be sure to peel it before eating – and the cheeks provide some of the best meat on an animal!

Once the head is finished, you can simply pull it apart with your hands and discard any bits that you do not want. You could make sausages with it, use it in a soup, or, of course, you can make head cheese – but we are not endeavouring there.

Serves 8
- ❖ **1 pig's head, cleaned (hair and glands removed)**
- ❖ **Sea salt (optional)**
- ❖ **Good charcoal**
- ❖ **Your preferred smoking wood (apple, cherry, oak, etc. – Saxon or Danish woods)**

You may want to soak the head in a brine before cooking, but it's not necessary. A simple salt brine works well, with any of your favourite flavourings added (see page 33).

Prepare your fire. You'll want to use a smoker here or a converted barbecue, but go ahead and oven roast if you prefer – cooking at 110–120°C/225–250°F/gas ¼–½ for about 5 hours, or until the cheeks are tender. Light a large chimney starter three-quarters filled with charcoal briquettes. When the top coals are partially covered with ash, pour the coals evenly over half of the barbecue and allow them to heat until almost white. Place wood chips or chunks on the coals, then set a cooking grate in place, cover the barbecue and open the lid vent completely. Heat until hot and the wood chips are smoking, about 5 minutes.

Brush clean and oil the cooking grate. Place the head, neck down, onto the grate. If you're looking for fancy presentation, wrap the ears in foil so they don't burn. Smoke for about 5 hours, then test for tenderness in the cheeks. Wrap the head in foil after you pull it from the smoker, let it rest for 10–15 minutes.

Meanwhile, heat the oven to 110–120°C/225–250°F/gas ¼–½. Once rested, transfer the head to the oven and continue to cook for about an hour. Pull apart, chop and enjoy! Great in sandwiches, or in pottage (see page 47).

Caraway Roasted Ribs

Very simple, very delicious. Spare ribs can be quite fatty but this will cook out, and as it does it bastes the meat and adds flavour. Caraway is an oft-overlooked seasoning for savoury meats, but it is very traditional in Saxon cooking. The caraway will hit your tongue and your mind, and you'll think you've mistakenly been spiked with henbane.

- ❖ **Racks of free-range pork spare ribs (½ rack per person)**
- ❖ **Salt and white pepper, to taste**
- ❖ **Caraway seeds, whole or freshly ground**

Preheat the oven to 140°C/275°F/gas 1.

The only trick here is to make sure you completely remove the membrane that lines the inside of the ribs, as not all butchers will do this prior to sale. Take a paring knife and cut a finger hold into the lining, then pull up and over with consistent pressure, pulling the membrane right off. Sometimes this can be tricky, but free-range animals tend to have thicker membranes that will pull off very easily. Discard the membrane.

Season well with salt and pepper, using white pepper if available, for an even bigger Germanic punch. Then sprinkle on your whole (or ground) caraway seeds, enough to cover the meat well. The whole seeds add a very nice texture and have a roasted flavour when cooking is complete. After sprinkling, press these flavourings onto the meat, noting the underside will hold less but should also be seasoned.

Roast in the oven for 3–4 hours, until tender, or as 'fall off the bone' as desired.

GARDEN

A Spring Pottage

Pottages and stews were part of the backbone of the Anglo-Saxon existence. Pottages – a common phrase in these times and through the later Medieval period – were more grain-centric, while stews were mainly meat-based. Both were cooked in a cauldron over the fire, and pottages used leftover bits of vegetables along with barley and wheat. Barley was the most plentiful grain and provided a rich supplement.

- ❖ Fat of choice, for frying
- ❖ 150g (5oz) onions, chopped
- ❖ 15g (½oz) chopped chives
- ❖ 15g (½oz) chopped mint
- ❖ 200g (7oz) barley
- ❖ 1 litre (33fl oz) good-quality stock of choice, bought or homemade (see page 123)
- ❖ 5 baby turnips, cut in half, or 1 good-sized turnip, cut into chunks
- ❖ 200g (7oz) mixed greens (turnip or carrot tops, kale, mustard leaves, cabbage, dandelion leaves)
- ❖ Salt and freshly ground black pepper

Set a pot over medium-high heat, spoon in the fat and heat it until it is shimmering. Add in the onions, chives, mint, and some salt and pepper and cook until the onions are translucent and the pepper fragrant.

Toss in the barley and lightly toast it, stirring occasionally, for 5 minutes. Pour in the stock, stirring, and add the turnips and the greens, then simmer for 30–40 minutes until the barley is done – as toothsome or as tender as you like.

Ale-glazed Carrots

Carrots were reddish-purple and small during Saxon times. In winter months, carrots are sweeter, but they could also have been glazed with beer in the Middle Ages because water was often polluted – which was why most people, even children, drank beer instead of water.

- **Bunch of fat carrots**
- **3 tablespoons butter or chicken fat**
- **250ml (8fl oz) ale (a pale ale works here, with its piney, malty flavour)**
- **Salt and freshly ground black pepper**

Peel the carrots and cut into thick rounds.

Melt the fat in a large pan, add the carrots, season with salt and black pepper and cook for a few minutes until lightly browned.

Pour in the ale, bring to a boil and reduce the heat so the liquid simmers. Cook the carrots until tender, about 20 minutes. The ale will reduce and be syrupy. If not, remove the carrots from the pan and boil the liquid until syrupy.

Parsnip Chips

Parsnips resemble carrots but are not edible raw. They develop their sweet taste when they are cooked. Look for firm, medium-sized parsnips, as large ones have a woody centre and small ones are too small after peeling to be used for chips.

- ❖ **3 parsnips**
- ❖ **1 tablespoon olive oil or chicken fat**
- ❖ **Salt and freshly ground black pepper**

Preheat the oven to 245°C/475°F/gas 9.

Peel and slice the parsnips as thinly as possible – slightly random widths is fine. Toss them in the fat, season with salt and pepper, and spread out on a baking sheet.

Roast for about 8 minutes, until the edges are starting to brown. Turn over and roast for another 8 minutes – some will be crispy but not burned, others just sweet.

Smothered Cabbage

Caraway seeds were well known in ancient Egypt and Rome. As early as 1500 BC the seeds were used as medicine and as a digestive aid. It was the Romans who brought the seeds to England.

This simple cabbage recipe, likely made by the Saxons, puts thickly sliced cabbage right onto the grate over a fire. You can also wrap it in foil with a bit of butter and salt.

Serves 6–8
- ❖ **Knob of butter, for frying**
- ❖ **1 cabbage, cored and thinly sliced**
- ❖ **Caraway seeds, to taste**
- ❖ **Salt and freshly ground black pepper**

Melt a knob of butter in a large pan over medium heat, add a little water and the sliced cabbage. Cover the pan and cook over medium-low heat until the cabbage is tender, about 20 minutes.

Remove the lid and let the liquid boil off, then season with caraway seeds, salt and black pepper. Serve warm.

Stuffed Cabbage

This is a simple dish that pulls together foods from a variety of sources to make a court-like dish – simple things elevated through application. It is also a good way to stretch out what meat one has. We use buckwheat here because it was common to Nordic and Germanic cultures and gives a floral taste and aroma as well as a better mouthfeel than rice. The mead and cherries provide a sweet and sour taste that's similar to modern braised tomato sauce. Use whatever cherry type you find – even dried. The buckwheat and the filling can be prepared the day before, which will also allow the flavours to meld.

Serves 8
- ❖ **1 green cabbage**
- ❖ **Fat of choice, for frying**
- ❖ **1 onion, diced**
- ❖ **185g (6½oz) buckwheat**
- ❖ **450g (1lb) minced veal**
- ❖ **450g (1lb) minced pork**
- ❖ **1 tablespoon dried or 15g (½oz) fresh marjoram**
- ❖ **138g (5oz) dried or 675g (1½lb) fresh cherries**
- ❖ **1 bottle of mead**
- ❖ **Salt and freshly ground black pepper**

Prepare the cabbage – a simple shortcut here is to freeze the head, then let it thaw. This will soften the leaves so that they are workable, without increasing the water content as blanching would. The same effect happens by leaving them out in a frost (uprooted, of course)! Just be certain the leaves are thawed before using.

Next, prepare the filling. Heat the fat in a casserole dish or large saucepan over medium heat. Add the onion to the pan, lightly salting, and cook until softened and translucent. Remove to a mixing bowl and let cool. Prepare the buckwheat according to the packet directions, then once cool add it to the mixing bowl. Add in the minced meats, marjoram, salt and pepper, and mix loosely with your hands. Let it sit to allow the flavours to combine – this can be left in the fridge overnight.

When ready to use, preheat the oven to 180°C/350°F/gas 4. Lay out a cabbage leaf and put about 2 heaped tablespoons of the meat mixture in the middle – how much is determined by how much the leaf can hold. Roll the leaves like little packages, folding the ends in. Place the packages in a pan or baking dish, seam side down.

Prepare the cherries – if fresh, stone and halve them, or chop as desired. If dried, roughly chop them. You can either combine these with mead in a small saucepan and cook on low for about 30 minutes to marry the flavours, or simply sprinkle the cherries on top of the packages and pour the bottle of mead over.

Cover the dish with a lid or foil and cook in the oven for 1 hour. If the mead is rather thin, remove the lid and cook for another 30 minutes or until it is reduced as you like.

Cabbage with Apples and Honey

❖ **2 tablespoons vegetable oil**
❖ **1 green cabbage, cored and sliced**
❖ **2 Granny Smith apples, peeled, cored and cut into chunks**
❖ **75ml (3fl oz) cider vinegar**
❖ **1 tablespoon honey, or less**
❖ **Caraway seeds, to taste, lightly toasted in a dry pan**
❖ **1 teaspoon salt**
❖ **Freshly ground black pepper, to taste**

In a large pot, heat the oil and add the cabbage, then cook for 1 hour, until soft and tender. Stir in the apples.

Combine the vinegar and honey in a small bowl and pour into the pot along with a good sprinkling of caraway seeds, the salt and a little black pepper. Cover with a lid and cook slowly, stirring occasionally, until very tender. The apples, with the long simmering, will break up.

Turnips

Pliny the Elder (died AD 79) considered the turnip one of the most important vegetables of his day, rating it 'directly after cereals or at all events after the bean, since its utility surpasses that of any other plant . . . this vegetable is not particular about the type of soil in which it grows and, because it can be left in the ground until the next harvest, it "prevents the effects of famine" for humans.'

Turnip Bisque

This bisque is wonderful served hot or cold, and is especially delicious smooth, so use a blender, if you have one. Choose turnips that feel heavy – older, less-tasty turnips are spongy in the middle and feel light. If they come with their greens, cut a few fronds and use these to garnish the soup.

- ❖ 2 tablespoons butter
- ❖ 4 large turnips, about 900g (2lb), peeled and roughly chopped
- ❖ 1 large onion, chopped
- ❖ 1 large leek, sliced
- ❖ 1 litre (33fl oz) chicken or vegetable stock, bought or homemade (see page 123)
- ❖ 120ml (4fl oz) double cream
- ❖ Pinch of salt

Heat the butter in a large saucepan. Add the turnips, onion, leek and a pinch of salt and cook over low heat until softened, 8–10 minutes.

Pour the stock over the vegetables and bring to a boil. Reduce the heat and simmer for 15 minutes until the turnips are soft.

Pour the soup into a serving dish or individual bowls and stir in the cream.

Braised Turnips

Turnips would have been a major root vegetable, with the benefit of their delicious greens on top. For this recipe, we halve young, smaller turnips, leaving the cleaned skin on along with a bit of the green stalks. Bay leaves give a delicious flavour and would have been known to the Saxons, but you could substitute this with your preferred herb. If you do, keep it light; this is all about the turnip.

If you want to stretch this dish, you could add an egg for a light soup, or for a more substantial version, add some boiled meat or fish on top of the bowl when serving.

- ❖ **12 young spring turnips**
- ❖ **4 medium turnips (if skin is thick, peel as desired)**
- ❖ **½ white or yellow onion, cut into quarters**
- ❖ **2 tablespoons butter or chicken, pork or beef fat**
- ❖ **3 bay leaves**
- ❖ **Salt and freshly ground black pepper**

Combine the vegetables, fat and bay leaves in a large saucepan with enough water to just cover, season, then simmer over low heat until cooked through, about 20 minutes. I often use the remaining liquid as a delicious dip for crusty or stale bread.

Pan-fried Turnips

- ❖ Chicken fat or olive oil, for frying
- ❖ Turnips, peeled if older, roughly chopped
- ❖ Salt

Heat the fat in a pan over medium heat until hot. Cook the turnips until brown on one side, about 15 minutes, then flip over onto the other side. Sprinkle with salt while warm so that the seasoning penetrates the turnips.

Smashed Turnips

- ❖ Turnips, peeled
- ❖ Butter, for greasing
- ❖ Salt and freshly ground black pepper

Preheat the oven to 200°C/400°F/gas 6.

Wrap each turnip in foil and add a knob of butter inside the foil packages. Bake for 45 minutes.

Remove the turnips from their packages. Place on a plate and smash the top down with a mallet (or potato masher). Sprinkle with salt and grindings of black pepper.

Raw Turnips

- ❖ Turnips, peeled and thinly sliced
- ❖ Coarse salt

Serve cold sliced turnips with a bowl of coarse salt.

Saxon Compote

This is a warrior's compote, with an ale to assist in the maceration. Perfect atop your morning pancakes or on a crust of bread with some cheese, and it's also a wonderful condiment for your roasted meats and game.

- ❖ **2 medium-sized apples (Fuji, Granny Smith – firm, sweet, tart), cored and roughly chopped (skin on)**
- ❖ **35g (1½oz) finely chopped walnuts**
- ❖ **Fat of choice**
- ❖ **5 heaping tablespoons good honey**
- ❖ **300ml (10fl oz) good brown ale, ESB (extra special bitter) style**
- ❖ **Salt and freshly ground black or white pepper**

Place the apples and walnuts in a saucepan that's big enough to hold all the ingredients over medium heat and bring to a low simmer. Spoon in the fat, then sprinkle in the salt and pepper, drizzle in the honey and pour over the ale. Stir to incorporate. Bring to a boil over medium heat, then lower the heat to a simmer, cover with a lid and simmer for 30 minutes. Remove the lid to reduce the ale to grant that malty flavour.

DAIRY AND BAKERY

Egg Cake

Pancakes are first mentioned around 600 BC. This one is an egg batter baked in the oven (like Yorkshire pudding). Three eggs make the pancake rise and fluff, which is intended and part of the pleasure. This is delicious topped with good local honey and more lard/schmaltz/suet/butter, as desired, or one of our compote recipes.

- ❖ **3 tablespoons fat (lard, schmaltz, suet or butter)**
- ❖ **3 eggs**
- ❖ **60g (2½oz) flour (consider rye, buckwheat, oat and, of course, whole wheat)**
- ❖ **¼ teaspoon salt**
- ❖ **120ml (4fl oz) whole milk**
- ❖ **Pinch of ground spice for flavouring – nutmeg, cinnamon or cloves**

Preheat the oven to 230°C/450°F/gas 8.

Drop the fat into an ovenproof cooking vessel (a 23cm/9in ovenproof frying pan is ideal, but any 15 x 15cm/6 x 6in or 15 x 23cm/6 x 9in dish works). This creates a wonderful base to quick-fry the bottom of the batter.

Mix all the egg cake ingredients together in a large bowl. Pour the batter into the pan, then transfer to the oven and bake for 15 minutes until set.

Frittata with Beef Crisps

A 'cake', or frittata, of eggs and meat scraps! This is delicious served with green sauce (see page 133) atop the eggs or chopped fresh herbs in a bit of good apple cider vinegar.

- ❖ **8 eggs**
- ❖ **1 onion**
- ❖ **Handful of meat trimmings, chopped (trimmed meat, or leftovers)**
- ❖ **Extra fat as needed, unless your meat scraps are on the fatter side**
- ❖ **Salt and freshly ground black pepper**

Crack the eggs into a large mixing bowl, add a pinch of salt, and whisk vigorously to combine.

Cut off the top of the onion, then halve the onion lengthwise and peel. Slice into thin 'half-moons'.

Add the meat to a frying pan over medium heat and cook until the fat from the scraps is mostly melted off or crisped, stirring occasionally. Add the onion slices and cook, stirring occasionally, until softened. Taste for seasoning and add more salt if needed, pepper if desired.

Gently pour in the beaten eggs, being sure to spread them evenly over the pan base. You want the meat and onions to be submerged within the eggs, or barely poking out. Place a plate or extra lid atop the pan and heat until the eggs are cooked through, 7–10 minutes. Keep an eye on them; if your hob tends to run on the hotter side, you may want to cook over medium-low. Once the top of the frittata has cooked, place a plate atop the pan, and flip the pan so the frittata is 'bottom side up' on the plate, revealing the appealing cooked bottom.

Slide onto your cutting board and carve into slices.

Bread

The following recipe combines a leaven and dried yeast used by the Anglo-Saxons. Flours today are completely different from those used by the Saxons, and this loaf will have a hearth-like, rustic flavour with the addition of a small amount of whole wheat flour. The dough has to rise four times, since we are making a brand-new leaven.

- ❖ **380g (13oz) bread flour, plus extra for dusting**
- ❖ **30g (1oz) whole wheat flour**
- ❖ **1 teaspoon dried yeast**
- ❖ **1 teaspoon honey**
- ❖ **1 teaspoon salt**

Make a leaven. In a large mixing bowl mix 135g (4½oz) of the bread flour, all of the whole wheat flour, the yeast and honey with 325ml (11fl oz) warm water. Stir until smooth. Set aside, covered with cling film for 1 hour, then chill overnight or for one full day.

Remove the leaven from the fridge and allow to come to room temperature, about 1 hour. Place the rest of the bread flour on top of the leaven. Cover with cling film and set aside to ferment for about 4 hours at room temperature.

Add the salt. Using a wooden spoon or your hands, mix the dough ingredients together. When the dough starts coming together, knead in the bowl for 5 minutes. It will be sticky. Let it rest for 20 minutes to make it easier to work with.

Turn out onto a floured board and knead for about 10 minutes, or as long as it takes to feel the dough change consistency – it will become smooth. Put the dough back into the bowl and cover with a cloth. Leave for an hour at room temperature to rise. Punch down the dough and let rise for another 45 minutes to 1 hour.

Turn the dough onto the floured board again and punch down. It will be sticky, but only use as much flour as necessary to make a round ball. Cover with a cloth and let rise for 1 hour.

Preheat the oven to 245°C/475°F/gas 9.

Slash the bread with a sharp knife, making two or three slashes, 1cm (½in) deep in the top of the dough. Bake for 10 minutes, reduce the temperature to 220°C/425°F/gas 7 and continue baking for 20–30 minutes. When the bread is properly cooked the loaf should sound hollow when rapped underneath. Leave to cool before slicing.

Rolls

You can use the dough recipe above to make rolls, too.

Cut the dough into 8–12 pieces, then roll each piece into a ball and place on flour-covered baking sheets. Cover with a cloth and let rise for 1 hour, or until the rolls are doubled in size.

Preheat the oven to 200°C/400°F/gas 6, then when hot bake the rolls for 20 minutes.

Unleavened Oatcakes

Pancakes are a cheap, quick everyday food, and even the Anglo-Saxons used large iron frying pans over open fires to make pancakes. These can be eaten any time of the day, served as a side with poultry or fish, or by themselves.

- ❖ 120ml (4fl oz) milk
- ❖ 125g (4½oz) quick-cooking oats
- ❖ 1 egg
- ❖ 2 tablespoons chopped parsley
- ❖ 1 small onion, chopped
- ❖ 60g (2½oz) butter
- ❖ Salt and freshly ground black pepper

Heat the milk in a small pan until boiling, then pour it over the oats in a heatproof bowl, stir, then let sit for 15 minutes. Stir in the egg, parsley and some salt and pepper.

Cook the onion in a frying pan with half the butter until softened, then add it to the oatmeal batter.

Heat the remaining butter on a griddle pan over medium heat. Using 1 tablespoon of batter per pancake, cook the pancakes one at a time until golden brown and crispy on both sides.

Barley Flatbread

Barley was cultivated 10,000 years ago. The Saxons used barley for brewing ale and for making flour. Anglo-Saxons could have made unleavened bread from flour, salt and water.

- ❖ **185g (6oz) barley flour, plus extra for dusting**
- ❖ **¼ teaspoon salt**
- ❖ **120ml (4fl oz) water**
- ❖ **1 tablespoon honey**

Mix the flour and salt together, then stir in the water and honey until a dough is formed.

Set a griddle or large frying pan on the hob over medium-high heat.

Put the dough on a lightly dusted worktop and knead it until it forms a smooth dough. This will take a few minutes. Roll the dough with a rolling pin until very thin, then cut circles from it using a large glass, pot lids or a knife traced around a small plate.

Place the pieces into the hot pan and cook for about 2 minutes per side until there are a few brown spots.

Serve plain, with honey and yogurt, or with cheese and meat.

King Alfred's Cakes

Crumpets are an Anglo-Saxon invention. At first, they were hard pancakes cooked on a griddle, like the recipe below, then centuries later baking powder was added, and later still yeast, which gave the characteristic holes and texture that crumpets became known for.

- ❖ **300g (10oz) oats**
- ❖ **60g (2½oz) oat flour**
- ❖ **175g (6oz) butter, melted**
- ❖ **35g (1½oz) dried fruit, coarsely chopped**
- ❖ **6 tablespoons honey**
- ❖ **½ teaspoon salt**

Set a griddle or frying pan on the hob over medium-high heat.

Mix all the ingredients together in a mixing bowl and form into 10–12 small patties.

Place the pieces onto the hot pan and cook for about 2 minutes per side until there is a slight char, pressing down with a rubber spatula to get the brown spots.

THE FIRST VICTORY

For this Home section, the story shows Uhtred as a child at Bebbanburg. Uhtred never recalls his early life with great pleasure, at least not until he was adopted by Ragnar. Nevertheless his first years show his eagerness to become a warrior who will fight with his brains as much as his brawn . . .

There is a general belief that all men remember their first woman. That is certainly not true of me, though I do remember the circumstances, I cannot remember exactly how old I was. I think twelve, but I could be wrong. It happened on the northern bank of the River Humber where Ragnar the Elder, who had adopted me as a son, was summoned to a great gathering of the Danish lords who had conquered Northumberland. I still remember the ships hauled onto a shingle beach, the tents, the great fires and the games that accompanied the gathering. There were tugs-of-war, simulated sword fights, some of which became all too real, horse races, and drinking competitions. When the contests were over the men gathered around a great fire to discuss matters of state and we children, too young to be allowed into those dull discussions, were told to tend the campfires, guard the horses and stay out of the way. Inevitably we played our own games, one of which was a vast hide-and-seek. One night I hid in a ship, beneath the steering platform at the stern, which proved a good place because it was raining and I had found good shelter and even some rough blankets in which I lay and listened to the voices searching nearby.

Two or three other boys found me and, liking my refuge, stayed hidden and gradually more arrived, both boys and girls, and I was pushed into the angle of the ship's stern where I sat, legs outstretched and my back leaning against the curved sternpost. I was comfortable, warm and dry, and gradually realised that the small compartment was getting exceedingly crowded and that my fellow refugees were not in the least concerned about staying silent. It was pitch dark in there, the rain clouds obscured whatever moon there might have been, and the beach was screened from the campfires by a stand of trees. I was happy enough, joining in the laughter when it came my way. No one bullied me or scorned my Saxon birth, indeed no one seemed aware of my presence.

And then the noise changed and a sense of excitement filled the crowded space. There was less laughter and more giggling, gasping and moaning. I wished I could see, but the darkness was absolute and I did not like to ask what caused the new noises, so stayed silent in my corner. Where I was suddenly seized. For a moment I thought someone was trying to wrestle me, but then a girl's voice said, close to my ear, 'Who are you?'

'Uhtred,' I said.

She was lying on top of me, having pulled herself up my body. 'And you're dressed!' she said, sounding surprised, even shocked.

'I am,' I responded feebly, then almost gasped myself because, in an attempt to ease her off my awkwardly pos-itioned body, I felt hers and discovered she was decidedly not dressed.

'Poor Uhtred,' she said, and proceeded to tug at my clothes.

I did eventually ask her name and I think she answered me, but I have long forgotten what it was, and by that time we were deep among a squirming mass of naked bodies and I cannot even be sure that the girl whose name I asked was even the same one who had first climbed onto me in the ship's stern. I think she was, and I have fond memories of her, so yes, I do remember her, but have not the faintest idea who she was.

But what I do remember, in sharp detail, is my first victory. Strangely, now that I am old, I remember the women and never think about the victories. The memories of the women bring me comfort, while the victories are sour with the stink of blood, the death of friends and the recollection of terror. Even my first victory had an element of terror, and that aspect was to grow bigger and come closer in the long wars that followed.

And that first victory all began with eels.

My father believed that eels were born when a horse shed hairs from its tail into a stream, and he loved eating eels so much that he would sometimes cut hairs from his stallion and throw them into the Ellewic, a stream that flowed north of Bebbanburg. He ate smoked eels, or else seethed in ale, all served on a great steaming platter.

I hated eels. Much later, after I had been captured by Ragnar the Dane who treated me as a son, I decided that eels were the spawn of Corpse-Ripper, the ghastly serpent who lives in Niflheim which is the icy hell that waits for vile people. One of the tasks given me by my father was to catch eels. I think he made me do it because he disliked me. In fairness he did not like any children, though he claimed to be fond of my elder brother who, he said, would grow to be a famous warrior. 'Whereas you,' he would say to me, 'will be good for nothing. Maybe you'll be a priest.'

I did not want to be a priest, but nor did I want to be an eel catcher, though I became good at it. Ealdwulf, Bebbanburg's smith, taught me how to trap them. 'Find some old fishing net, boy,' he told me, 'then bring it here.'

Here was his smithy, a smoky, dirty hut in Bebbanburg's

lower courtyard where I liked to watch Ealdwulf hammer red-hot iron into spearheads or sword-blades. He seemed to like me, especially when I went scavenging on Bebbanburg's graveyard that lay just to the south of the fortress. A high tide and a strong eastern gale would sometimes uncover the graves and I would bring him bones that he put on the furnace. 'No one knows why, boy,' he told me, 'but add bones to the fire and the iron gets stronger. It becomes *stehl*, and the best blades are *stehl* blades.' He liked to use human bones because he reckoned they had more sorcery than the plentiful bones of cattle or sheep.

He was a pagan, though he wore a scorched wooden cross simply because everyone else in Bebbanburg was a Christian and because my father had insisted, though I am not sure why because I suspected my father was secretly a pagan himself. He sometimes boasted that our family was descended from Woden. 'We have the blood of gods!' he would proclaim, and Gytha, his second wife and my stepmother, would bleat an impotent protest and touch the silver cross that hung between her breasts.

'Enough fishing net to cover my anvil, boy,' Ealdwulf told me, and I obediently searched through the tide wrack in the harbour to discover a scrap of tarred twine-net that I brought to him. 'Now go and dig worms, boy,' he said. He gave me a clay jug about the size of his big fire-scarred hand. 'Fill that.'

That, at least, I knew how to do. I went to the vegetable fields behind the village that lay on the far side of Bebbanburg's shallow harbour, found a damp spot that was thick with leaf mould, and dug into the soil. It took the best part of a morning to fill the jug with worms, which I then carried back to the smithy.

'Now watch,' Ealdwulf said.

He lay the net on a table and rolled the worms inside to make a tube that he bundled into a rough ball which he lashed with twine. He left a long tail of twine as a handle.

'Take that to the Ellewic after dark,' he told me, 'and throw it in the water. Take a rake or a fish-spear and a bucket to bring the buggers back. You'll get plenty!'

'After dark?' I asked nervously.

'Doesn't work in the daylight,' he told me, 'don't know why, just doesn't. Probably sorcery. But do it at night, lad, and the eels will swarm all over that bundle of worms.'

He was right. I stood knee-deep in the Ellewic stream, threw the worm bundle into the moonlit water, and within minutes I was scooping eels onto the bank. Eels thrashed and writhed about the bait, wriggling as close as those young bodies years later in the long ship by the Humber, and I scooped them from the stream with a rake, then chased them through the long grass. I picked them up and they would coil themselves around my arm as I pushed them into a barrel. I was eight years old and had a struggle to carry the barrel back to the fortress where Kenric, one of Bebbanburg's most experienced warriors, commanded the guard on the Low Gate. It was always the Low Gate back then. It was my treacherous uncle who, when he stole the fortress from me, began to decorate the gate with skulls, so giving it the new name, Skull Gate.

'What you got, boy?' Kenric asked me.

'Eels.'

'Let's have a look, eh?'

He was a lean, sinewy man who had the reputation of being quick as a striking snake in battle. He was a battle companion of Ælfric, my father's younger brother who lived with us in Bebbanburg, and even as a child I sensed that Ælfric resented that he was the younger brother and so had not inherited the fortress. Kenric probably encouraged that resentment, but that night he seemed pleasant enough as he took the barrel from me, prised open the lid and gave a low whistle of surprise. 'A good night's hunting, boy! I'll have one of those for breakfast.' He lifted out a long, yellow-green eel. 'Does your father pay you for his eels?'

'I hope he will,' I said, watching as Kenric sliced off the eel's head with a knife. The decapitated body went on wriggling.

'He'll give you silver?' Kenric asked.

'I hope so,' I said, though in truth my father seldom rewarded me, but once or twice he had given me a battered copper coin when he was in a rare good mood.

'You'll be rich after this night's catch,' Kenric said, then let me put the lid back on the barrel and watched as I staggered under its heavy weight towards the inner gate.

My father was pleased. He even went to the kitchens to see the eels. 'You caught all these?'

'Yes, Father.'

'Not as useless as he looks!' he said to the women working at the big stone oven, and gave me a silver shilling, which, for him, was outrageously generous. 'Get me more, boy, we'll have an eel feast.' He picked out the biggest eel, a silver-skinned fat beast, which writhed desperately in his grip. He pinned it to the wall with a knife thrust just beneath its head, then drew a shorter knife from his belt, slashed the skin twice, then ripped the skin clean off. 'That'll make a nice belt,' he said, then nodded to one of the women. 'Fry the rest of that one for a midday meal.' He slapped me around the head. 'Well done, boy. Bring more and I'll pay you well.'

I liked his praise, which was more valuable to me than the silver shilling he had given me, which, in truth, was scarcely useful at all. I had nowhere to spend it, and so I added it to the small hoard of copper coins I kept hidden in the gallery of the great hall where I slept.

Next morning, after a breakfast of grease-smeared bread and small ale, I started my chores.

My father insisted my brother and I worked, though my elder brother was given the cleaner tasks like supervising the constant repairs to Bebbanburg's great timber ramparts. My first job every morning was to feed my father's beloved wolf-hounds and, when that was done, I had to catch horse piss in a bucket, then use the piss to polish silver. When my chores were finished Father Beocca, my father's priest, would take me for lessons, teaching me to read and to write and to learn the saints' lives. I liked Beocca, but would rather have been scrubbing silver plates with sand and horse piss than listen to his tales of holy men preaching to seals and puffins.

'Do puffins go to heaven?' I asked him once.

'They are God's creatures,' he assured me, 'all of God's creatures will go to heaven.'

'Dogs?'

'Heaven is unimaginable without dogs,' he answered with a smile.

'What about mosquitoes?'

He had sighed and pointed at his book. 'Read me that word.'

At mid-morning it was time for lessons in sword-craft. All the boys were expected to train with wooden swords and half-sized shields, and I usually enjoyed it because, like most small boys, I was fascinated by the tales of warriors. At night I would often creep to the edge of the gallery and listen as a harpist chanted a tale of war, and I would hear my father's men roar their approval and hammer the table as the stories unfolded. Those tales were always glorious, how some warrior had cut down the enemy with his sword, or broken a shield wall, or turned a wheat field into a quagmire of blood. They never told of dying men calling for their mothers, or the stink of shit as men fouled themselves in terror. The enemy was usually the Scots, but then the Danes came, and even Father Beocca, who had long taught me that war was a sad necessity, became belligerent. 'They are the enemies of Christ,' he told me, 'turds of Satan! Pagans! Heathens! Learn your sword-skills, boy, learn them well!'

All we boys began with wooden swords, learning to cut and lunge, usually fighting each other, but sometimes we were matched against my father's warriors, who liked to hammer us unmercifully.

'Harden them!' my father would growl. He never enquired of Father Beocca whether I was learning my letters, but he often watched me at sword practice and would sometimes pick up a wooden sword and dare me to attack him. I always did, and always ended bruised and on the ground, once with a broken rib.

'If you can't fight, boy, you're useless,' he snarled, then told Deogol, who was his chief warrior, to match me against bigger boys. 'He has to learn! Make sure he does.'

I always hated the moment when Deogol told us to choose sides. In the year of the eel hunts I was eight years old, one of the youngest boys, and as often as not I was among the very last to be picked. Sometimes, because I was my father's son and my father was Lord of Bebbanburg, I was picked first, but that choice was always greeted with jeers because the other boys, almost all of them older, believed I was only chosen early to earn favour with my father. But more often than not I was among the last two or three to be picked.

'You're no use, Squeaker,' Grindan told me, 'you're too small, too slow, too stupid.'

Grindan never picked me, but liked to fight me because he was older, bigger and faster. He called me Squeaker, because he claimed that was the noise I made when he hit me with one of the wooden training swords.

Grindan was Kenric's son, a boy of thirteen, almost old enough to join the grown warriors, and he led a group of boys his own age who boasted that they would become Bebbanburg's most feared fighters, and they enthusiastically trained with swords, spears and shields to make that boast come true. All of them took a perverse delight in hurting me.

'It's for your own good, boy,' my father claimed when he saw me with a broken scalp and blood-soaked hair. 'You'll be useless if you can't fight.'

'He could become a priest,' Gytha suggested hopefully.

'That's what I said,' my father retorted, 'he'll be useless.'

On the morning after my first successful eel hunt I was matched against Grindan again. We were being taught how to use axes, though again our weapons were made of wood.

'You hook the axe over your enemy's shield,' Deogol explained, 'and pull it down. Then the man next to you kills the pagan bastard. Now try it!'

We flailed away, working with a partner who was supposed to lunge a spear or sword when we had successfully dragged the opponent's shield down, though I was not strong enough to move Grindan's shield. For once he did not take advantage to whack me about the head with his wooden axe.

'So your father paid you for eels?' he asked.

'He did.'

'How much?'

'Enough,' I grunted as I tried to pull his shield down.

'Silver?'

'Enough,' I said again, tugging vainly at his shield.

'Where do you find eels?'

'In a stream,' I said unhelpfully, then grunted again.

'You're too weak, Squeaker.' He grinned and raised his shield, forcing my arm up. I tried to kick him under his shield, but only managed a glancing blow on his shin that amused him. 'And I hear he wants more eels?' he asked. 'For a feast?'

'I hate eels,' I said, then used all my strength to haul his shield down, but the wooden axe slipped and ran around the edge, and he slammed his shield into mine, throwing me backwards.

'You're pathetic, Squeaker. You'll die in your first battle!' He thumped his axe against my shield, driving me back another pace. He was big for his age, with a broad, round face disfigured by his left cheek that was scarred by a dog-bite. He was proud of the scar, thinking it made him look like a seasoned warrior. He had been baiting the dog, one of my father's wolfhounds, and it had lunged at him and might even have killed him if his father had not beaten the hound away. Kenric had not dared kill the dog because my father adored his hounds, which had the freedom of Bebbanburg, fouling the great hall and snarling at anyone who tried to curb them. Grindan had been scared of the hounds ever since his cheek had been ravaged, but the hounds liked me. Some evenings I would curl into a corner of the hall and two or three of the big dogs would find me and lie down beside me. Bana, his name meant killer, was the lead dog, a fearless, grey-haired hound with scarred flanks who sometimes licked my face as I hid in the hall's shadow.

'So are you hunting for more eels, Squeaker?' Grindan demanded, hammering my shield with his wooden axe.

'If my father wants them, yes.' I tried to hook his shield again, but he pulled it back too quickly.

'That's all you're good for,' Grindan sneered. 'We'll be killing Danes and you'll be an eel-hunter!'

That afternoon I dug more worms and used the same stretch of tattered net to roll them into a squirming ball. I left the fortress at dusk, carrying the barrel, bait and rake, and Kenric was again commanding the Low Gate.

'Off again, boy?'

'I'll be back late,' I told him.

'We might let you back in.' He grinned, then slammed the gate shut behind me.

I went back to the Ellewic stream, going slightly further towards the sea, then waited for darkness. I was nervous of the darkness beyond the fortress because Father Beocca sometimes told me fearful tales of the sceadugengan, the night-walkers, who he said were creatures of Satan, shape-shifters, stalkers of the darkness and the enemies of Christians. 'They want your soul, boy, and if they find you they'll strip the flesh from your bones and carry your soul to the devil. Always wear the cross, boy, especially at night! The night is the devil's playtime.'

Yet I discovered I liked being alone in the whispering sea wind, high enough in the hills to gaze at the long silvery reflections of the rising moon on the glittering waters. I was a dreamer. My father often cuffed me around the head to wake me. 'No good thinking, boy, it's doing that counts! Thinking is for women.' For a while that second night I stayed on the higher ground, just watching the sea, listening to the small night sounds and wondering about my future. My brother would inherit Bebbanburg, and where would that leave me? Father Beocca wanted me to become a priest, but my father reckoned my probable destiny was to become some great lord's warrior. His younger brother, my uncle Ælfric, told me to conquer my own lands. 'That's how it's done, boy. Gather some friends, sharpen your swords, and take what you want!'

'You never did that, uncle,' I said once, puzzled.

'In time, boy, in time,' he had said, and in time he had taken Bebbanburg from me, but that treachery lay three or four years in the future after my father and brother were both dead. That night I imagined myself as a warrior in some other lord's service until the call of a nearby owl startled me from my thoughts and I went down to the stream and threw in my bundle of worms to start the eels thrashing again.

I filled the barrel, then carried it back down the track that led to the village. Bebbanburg was in front of me, rearing on its great lump of rock, the ramparts flaring with light where sentries had flaming torches that reflected from the shallow harbour. The eels were heavy and I staggered under their weight. On the lower ground, where a grove of windswept trees grew to the north of the village, I put the barrel down and rested. I could hear the eels moving and wondered how many I would need if my father were to give a feast for all his warriors, and how much he would pay me, and it was then, while I was resting, that I heard the sceadugengan.

Shadow-walkers! It was the crack of a twig, a footfall, and I looked around, but the trees were dark with shadows thrown by the moon. I was in shadow too, and stayed there, my heart beating hard, my hand on the hilt of the small knife sheathed at my belt. I knew the sceadugengan were the dead. Father Beocca had told me they were the souls of sinners who came from the graveyards at night to seek revenge on the living. I knew I should clutch the cross that hung around my neck, but the knife was more comforting, though what use a small blade would be against a creature that was only half alive

I did not know. I did pray. In those days I was a Christian, scared into a belief in the nailed god because I knew no better, and I sent a desperate silent prayer into the sky that the sceadugengan would not see me. Except that the eel-barrel lay in the centre of the path where I had left it, it was lit by the moon, and I feared it would attract them. I listened, heard nothing except the rustle of leaves and the endless pounding of the waves on the beach beyond the fortress.

I stood, waited again, still heard nothing, and so went back to the barrel. I was about to lift it when the sceadugengan erupted from the shadows, except they were not shadow-walkers, they were three boys, two of whom slammed me back onto the path. One of them hit me around the head, so that for a moment I was dizzy, hardly aware that I was being kicked hard until a sharp pain in my chest made me cry aloud.

'Leave him,' a voice said, 'I hope it hurt, Squeaker.'

One of the boys kicked me again, they laughed, and then they were gone, the eel-barrel with them.

It had been Grindan, of course. I had recognised his voice, and the voices of his friends who, like Grindan, only dreamed of being household warriors who could stand in the shield wall and boast of their prowess.

I was hurting. There was blood in my mouth and one of my teeth felt loose, my ribs were agony, but I managed to stand and stagger down the path, then stopped.

Kenric was guarding the Low Gate. He must have known his son had followed me, he had probably encouraged the ambush, and I did not want him to see me bloodied and bruised, did not want to hear his scornful laughter, and so instead I walked painfully down to the beach that lay north of the fortress. The tide was swirling into the narrow channel that led to the harbour, but I had swum it often enough and still had the big wooden rake that would help keep me afloat. I waded into the strong current, flinching from the pain in my ribs, then kicked my way across the channel. I was shivering as I climbed the southern bank, then hammered the rake's handle on the Sea Gate.

'Who in God's name are you?' a sleepy voice shouted from the ramparts.

'Osbert!' I called back, sounding squeaky and frightened. I was called Osbert then because the eldest son always took the name Uhtred, and my elder brother was still months away from his death at the hands of the Danes.

'Good Christ, boy, look at you?' The gate was opened by Wulfgar, a younger warrior who sometimes helped teach us sword-skill. 'Daft time to go swimming! Get yourself inside.' He peered at me. 'What happened?'

'I fell,' I said.

'Shouldn't go wandering in the night, boy. There are ghouls out there!' He said nothing more as I climbed the steep rock steps.

I just wanted my bed, but before I could reach the great hall and climb the ladder to the gallery my father saw me. He was coming from the lower courtyard, and called to me.

'What in Christ's name are you doing?'

'I was eel-fishing,' I said.

He tilted my head up. 'You're crying?'

'It's nothing, Father.'

'Men don't cry,' he said. 'Where are the eels?'

'Grindan stole them!' I blurted.

He paused, then chuckled. 'I just paid him silver!' He tugged me by the shoulder. 'Come on, lad, let's get you warm.'

'It's not fair!' I cried back.

'Of course it's not fair, don't be pathetic. Life isn't fair.' He led me into the hall, close to the great fire that was dying. 'I don't want to breed weaklings,' he said. 'So you've got an enemy. Show me you can deal with him. And I want more eels!'

'I'll kill him!' I blurted out.

'You won't, boy. Give him a good kicking, that's enough. Now go dry yourself at the hearth.'

I slept badly that night, still chilled from my damp clothes and more intent on imagining a revenge against Grindan than sleeping. In those waking dreams I beat him to pulp, sliced him with a seax, made him whimper, but that is all they were; waking dreams. He was too big, too strong, and I knew it.

Next day Father Beocca was making me read aloud from his copy of the life of Saint Hilda, a woman who had founded a nunnery at Witebia. 'A most holy woman,' he told me enthusiastically, 'and you can learn much from her!'

'She turned snakes to stone?'

'She did!'

'Can you do that?'

'God has not granted me that power.'

'Why not?'

'I was at Witebia once,' he changed the subject, 'and when the gulls fly over Saint Hilda's church they fold their wings in her honour! I saw it!'

'Did they fall from the sky?' I asked eagerly, imagining a church covered with dead seagulls.

'Of course not! They fold their wings in homage, and God lifts them.' I was disappointed in his answer and it must have shown because Beocca touched my shoulder. 'What's the matter, boy?'

'I have an enemy,' I confessed, 'and have to fight him.'

'Nonsense! You must forgive him!'

'My father says I must fight him.'

Beocca was ever unwilling to contradict my father, who paid him. He made the sign of the cross.

'Tell me, boy,' he said unhappily. So I told him the story of my eel hunt, and how Grindan and his two companions had ambushed me. The shame of it still rankled and there were tears in my eyes.

'And I must go back tonight!' I wailed. 'My father wants more eels.'

'You shouldn't be out of the fortress after dark,' Beocca said, 'it isn't safe!'

'I have to fetch the eels! And they're only there at night.'

'Then you must pray, boy, you must pray. Come, we'll go to the chapel and beg God's help.'

In those days Bebbanburg's chapel was in the upper courtyard close to the granaries and storehouses. Much later, after I recaptured the fortress, I rebuilt it on the higher rock beside the great hall. I was a pagan by then, but at least half of my men were Christians and I gave them the new chapel as a reward for their loyalty, but in my childhood the chapel was lower down. It was a wooden building with a thatched roof that let in the rain and had a floor of soggy rushes. The altar was wooden and beneath it, in a silver box, was Bebbanburg's greatest treasure, the arm of Saint Oswald. Oswald had been King of Northumbria and, so Beocca never tired of telling me, a great Christian warrior.

'We shall pray to Saint Oswald and beg his protection for you,' he told me when we reached the chapel. 'His arm is uncorrupted!'

'What does that mean?' I asked.

'After death,' Beocca said as he tugged the precious reliquary from beneath the altar, 'our bodies decay. Maggots and worms eat us, though at the day of resurrection we shall be miraculously made whole again! But a saint's body never decays!'

'Truly?' I asked.

'Truly!' Beocca said, and fumbled with the latches of the silver reliquary which was a long box about the length of a sword-blade. 'On your knees,' he instructed me, and I obediently knelt as he reverently opened the lid.

The box was lined with pale linen that had been discoloured where the saint's arm lay. The arm was clothed in a sleeve embroidered with crosses, and from its cuff protruded a dark grey hand with skinny fingers curled like claws. The fingernails were black, the fingers themselves very thin and covered with dark skin.

'Behold,' Beocca said in a voice filled with awe, 'the arm of the blessed Saint Oswald. Now close your eyes and we shall both pray.'

I half closed my eyes while Beocca, his hands clasped before him, prayed that the saint would intercede with Almighty God to give me strength, and as he prayed I became aware of a movement behind me. I half turned and saw Bana, the big hound, had come into the chapel. The dog caught my eye, his tail wagged, then he padded forward on his great paws and lowered his head to sniff the arm.

'Grant him courage!' Beocca's closed eyes were pointed at the chapel's roof. 'Give your servant Osbert strength in his time of trial!'

Bana picked up the arm and backed away. The embroidered sleeve scraped on the box's edge and the small noise was enough to alert Beocca, who yelped in alarm and snatched at the arm, but Bana swerved away and trotted towards the chapel's open door.

'No!' Beocca cried, scrambling to his feet. I was laughing. 'Come!' Beocca struck my shoulder. 'Come!'

'Bana!' I shouted. 'Down!' And the big hound stopped, turned, and sat obediently as Beocca carefully took the sacred relic from his jaws.

'Oh dear God, forgive me,' Beocca said, carrying the arm back to its reliquary. He laid it on the linen, closed the lid and slid the latches into place. 'You will not tell anyone of this,' he warned me.

'My father should know,' I said mischievously.

'No! No! It is our secret! The arm is undamaged. No harm is done. You must say nothing! Promise me!' Poor Beocca was trembling at the awful thought that Bebbanburg's holy relic had so nearly become a snack for a wolfhound. 'Promise me!' he pleaded. He was frightened of my father's anger.

My father was not a pious Christian, but he was perversely proud of the relic, which brought pilgrims to Bebbanburg. 'Of course,' my father was fond of saying, 'Oswald was a piss-poor warrior. Spent too much time on his knees and not enough learning to fight.' Gytha would make feeble protests at this impiety, which only spurred my father to more scornful remarks about what a failure King Oswald had been. 'The useless bugger was defeated! Still,' he would go on, 'he's useful now! Brings us money!' The money came from pilgrims eager to pray for the saint's help and who always dropped coins into the big urn placed close to the chapel's altar.

'I'll say nothing,' I promised Beocca.

'And God and Saint Oswald will reward you,' he said, relieved. 'And dogs should not be permitted in the chapel!'

'You told me dogs go to heaven,' I said.

'They are God's creatures.'

'Then they should be allowed in church,' I insisted.

'Not if they eat saints,' Beocca said grimly. 'Close the door.'

He made me stay for a long time while he prayed, but either God or Saint Oswald had already suggested an answer to my predicament. I knew Grindan would wait for me again, along with his companions, and I knew that my friends were as frightened of Grindan as I was. He was simply too big and well-muscled to be fought. I needed allies, but those allies had to be as strong as Grindan and his friends.

That afternoon I left the fortress by the Sea Gate and scrambled across the rock and along the beach before walking across the neck of land that led to the Low Gate. I took that long way around so no one would see me. Once on the neck I would be visible to the men guarding the Low Gate, though I hoped they would think nothing of it. I went up into the woods where I had been ambushed, spent a few minutes there before digging more worms at the edge of the trees, then returned to the fortress through the Low Gate. None of the sentries said anything except to greet me.

I used the netting to tie the worms into a tight ball and left it inside the barrel, which I collected after dark, and, with the rake, carried into the night. Kenric was again commanding the Low Gate's guard.

'Eel-hunting again?' he asked me.

'My father wants more,' I said.

'Take care,' he said, grinning. He knew his son would follow me again, and knew, too, that my father would pay silver for the eels.

The gate slammed behind me, but I did not hear the locking bar fall into place and guessed that Kenric would only bar the gate once his son had slipped into the dark behind me.

I crossed the moon-silvered sandy neck, skirted the village, and followed the path that led north through the trees to the Ellewic, where I dropped the worm ball into a pool and listened to the eels thrash as they took the bait. I filled the barrel, hammered the top shut with the rake's handle, staggered back down the path, and finally dropped the barrel a few yards short of where I had stopped on the night Grindan had attacked me. Again there was moonlight, enough to reveal the barrel, which I left on the path as I slipped off into the shadows.

And again the sceadugengan came. Three of them, creeping up the path and carrying staves. 'The earsling has run away,' one said.

'Squeaker!' Grindan called. 'Where are you?'

'He's frightened!'

'Squeaker! You pathetic piece of shit! Where are you?'

I crouched, said nothing.

'He's run off,' one of Grindan's friends said. 'And we have his eels.'

'Pick it up,' Grindan ordered his companions, who lifted the barrel and then they all set off back through the trees. I could hear them laughing.

But I had been here earlier. I had left by the Sea Gate and walked all around the fortress leading Bana and another hound on long leather leashes. I was permitted to take two dogs out of the fortress to run them on the beach where they chased gulls and loved to splash in the small waves. I had taken a risk leading them across the sandy neck that was in full view of the southern ramparts, but no one had said anything when I returned without the hounds, which I had left tethered to a stunted oak in the woods. I had also left them a clay bowl filled with water. Now, after dropping the heavy eel-barrel, I had found the two dogs, fed them each a handful of tripe that I had stolen from the kitchens, then waited until the sceadugengan approached.

I waited till Grindan and his companions were going back towards the fortress, then I untied the leashes from the tree and followed. I could see them in the dappled moonlight some forty paces away, could still hear their laughter.

'Grindan, you earsling!' I shouted. 'Bring me my eels!'

The pair carrying the barrel put it down as Grindan turned.

'Squeaker! You want the eels? Come and get them!'

'I'm coming!' I called, and walked slowly towards them.

I had been in shadow, and the dogs, crouching either side of me, were dark. Grindan had not seen them and the first he knew of them was when we walked into a patch of moonlight. Bana was growling, tugging at his leash. He was a warrior, that dog.

'No!' Grindan said.

'You brought two friends,' I said, 'and so did I.'

I had stopped some six or seven paces from them, and both hounds were growling and pulling at the leashes. Grindan was holding the stave in front of him, watching Bana.

'You can have the eels,' he said.

'And you can carry them,' I said.

'We're going,' he snarled.

'And the dogs can run faster then you,' I said, and I let Bana's leash slip through my hand and the big hound leaped forward and I only just held onto the leash's end. 'He can't wait,' I said, 'and he's hungry. Pick up the barrel.'

'You wouldn't dare, Squeaker!' Grindan said defiantly.

I dared. I let go of Bana's leash and the dog sprang.

Grindan screamed. He forgot the stave, just turned to run, but before he had gone one pace Bana's jaws clamped on his right arm and Grindan screamed again as he was hauled down.

'Down, Bana! Back!' I shouted.

Grindan was on the path and Bana was standing over him, spittle dribbling from his open jaw onto Grindan's face. I stroked Bana's back, then took the leash and pulled him away.

'I told you to pick up the barrel,' I said, 'so do it.'

'He bit me!'

'He'll kill you if I let him,' I said, 'now carry the eels.'

He carried them down the path, along the village street that edged the harbour and across the sandy neck. His two companions walked alongside, giving nervous glances at the two hounds who still pulled menacingly at their leashes. One of Grindan's friends knocked on the Low Gate that Grindan's father unbarred and pulled open.

'To the kitchens, Grindan,' I said.

'He bit me!' Grindan appealed to his father. 'The dog, he bit me.'

'He'll bite you again if you don't take the eels to the kitchens,' I said.

Kenric looked at me, looked at the two dogs. I gave Bana a few inches of leash and he surged forward, teeth bared.

'Take the eels to the kitchen,' Kenric told his son.

'He hurt me!' Grindan jerked away from the hound.

'Not half as badly as he wants to,' I said.

'Go, boy,' Kenric said. I could see he wanted to punish me, but he was frightened of what my father would do in return. 'Just go!' he snarled.

We walked to the kitchens where Grindan obediently dropped the barrel and then fled to the huts where the families of the household warriors slept.

I had half thought my father might appear, but he did not

come, and so I returned the two hounds to their pen and then went to the great hall and climbed to the gallery where I finally fell asleep.

Next morning I fed the hounds as usual, polished silver and endured an hour or more of Beocca's teaching, and then picked up my practice wooden shield and wooden sword and went to the upper courtyard where Deogol matched me against Grindan.

'Straight fighting this morning,' Deogol announced. 'One man against one!'

'I'll kill you, Squeaker,' Grindan hissed at me.

'Shields up!' Deogol called. 'And start!'

Grindan began by hammering his shield into mine, using his weight and height to thrust me backwards. He followed it with a massive swing with his wooden sword that clattered on my shield, then another heavy thrust of his shield. I made a feeble lunge that was stopped by his shield and I saw he was going to swing his sword again in an attempt to throw my shield aside and so leave my body open to a powerful thrust. I swung my shield left to catch the blow, which jarred on the edge hard enough to dent the wood, but Grindan's right arm was extended and I brought my own sword hard down, across my body, to strike his forearm where Bana had bitten him the night before. There was a ragged rent in his sleeve marking the spot, and my sword struck it hard.

Grindan yelped. He stepped back, and I thrust my shield at him, pushing him back a pace, then stepped to my left and back-handed the wooden blade so that it again struck his wounded arm, and again he yelped, this time so loud that Deogol noticed and hurried to separate us.

'What's the matter?' he asked Grindan.

'My arm's broken! The little bastard set his dogs on me.'

91

'Let me look,' Deogol said, and made Grindan pull up his sleeve.

Bana had drawn blood that was now crusted in two or three places, and the scabs were surrounded by a great black bruise. I grinned in satisfaction as Deogol ran his hand down the wounded arm. Grindan cried out in pain as Deogol's hand slid over the bruise. 'Nothing broken,' he said dismissively, 'you can fight on.'

'I can't . . .' Grindan began.

'Fight!' Deogol snarled, and pushed Grindan towards me, and Grindan raised his sword, offering me another chance to hit his arm which I did, hard. My wooden sword slammed onto his bruised arm and he yelped again, loudly, and this time he dropped the sword in his pain and I lunged my own blade and struck him just above the belly so he bent over, crying, and I slapped the flat of my blade twice more on the bruised arm, then, for good measure, gave the arm a great scything blow and heard the bone crack. He screamed then, and his friends just looked on, astonished, and I felt the joy of victory.

'Enough!' Deogol stepped between us. 'Osbert wins.'

That night there was ale-seethed eels for supper and my father pointedly chucked a succulent lump to Bana. 'A most excellent hound,' he announced to the hall.

Grindan never did become a warrior; his arm set badly and he could neither wield a sword nor hold a shield, and so my father found him a job in the stables. He died young and unhappy.

It was my first victory.

Part Two

LAND AND WATER

Historical Background

Much of the food eaten by the Anglo-Saxons was found through foraging in the wider fields and woods, and also by fishing, both in the rivers and the nearby seas.

The land was plentiful in wild berries. Sloes, plums, black-berries, raspberries, elderberries, hawthorn berries, cherries, sour cherries, bullace (a type of plum), cloudberries, straw-berries, crab apples, rose hips and rowan berries could all be easily found. Some vegetables that are now considered domestic were also picked in the wild, like fennel and celery, as well as almost all herbs, which were used not only for adding flavour to dishes, but for medicinal purposes too. Nature freely provided cobnuts, hazelnuts, chestnuts and walnuts, which were an important source of protein and easy to store. And, of course, mushrooms could also be foraged in the nearby woods.

Fish was an important part of the diet, sometimes caught locally in the rivers, or often by those who lived near the sea, though few of these people could afford to own their own boats. Trout and eels were both fairly accessible and eaten quite widely, particularly by those who lived close to rivers and lakes. Salmon was rarer, but those Saxons who lived close by the sea would have had salt-water fish and shellfish in their diets too.

The foods grown, caught and eaten by the Anglo-Saxons and invading Vikings seem to have merged quite easily, based on what was available. The place where Uhtred was raised and lived was, for most of his life, ruled by Danish or Norse kings. Although he may have held on to his own lands, it was a small enclave in Viking territory. Even when eventually defeated by the southern Saxon kings, many of the Northmen stayed in the lands they had conquered and became assimilated into the local population. In time, the English language adopted some of the old Norse words, including those relating to food – what we now call 'eggs' (an old Norse word) were known as *eai* to the Anglo-Saxons, and, interestingly, both words were simultaneously in use during the early Middle Ages.

There is never much time for elaborate meals in Uhtred's complex life, but there is one: 'There was a feast three days after the battle . . . There was more ale than food, and what food there was did not taste good. There was bread, some hams, and a stew I suspected was horse-flesh . . . It was called a victory feast, and I suppose it was, but until the ale had loosened men's tongues, it felt more like a funeral.'

Such was the feast to celebrate the battle that created a united England!

Recipes

ANIMALS

Rabbit Braised in Ale ✛ Royal Beef Stew ✛ Brisket Hash ✛ Braised Lamb Shank ✛ Spatchcocked Chicken ✛ Meatballs from Three Animals ✛ Grilled Liver ✛ Juniper-spiced Boar Meatballs ✛ Pluck Hash ✛ Quail, two ways ✛ Braised Beef Brisket ✛ Venison Stew ✛ Stocks

WILD VEGETABLES

Cream-braised Leeks ✛ Beetroots, two ways ✛ Braised Greens ✛ Fennel, two ways ✛ Dandelion Salad with Bacon ✛ A Green Sauce ✛ Foraged Mushroom Omelette ✛ Sage and Pepper Omelette ✛ Chanterelle Toast

WATER

Grilled Trout ✛ Eel Pie ✛ Pickled Herring ✛ Kettle of Fish ✛ Oyster Stew ✛ Haddock Simmered in Ale ✛ Salmon, various ways ✛ Turbot, two ways

ANIMALS

Rabbit Braised in Ale, with Leeks and Fennel

The Romans reared rabbits for food and it is believed by some that they brought these animals to England for sport. However, other research says rabbits were not found in Britain until the Norman conquests. Hares and small deer were definitely around in Anglo-Saxon times, though, and can be cooked like rabbits. Choose your preferred animal for this casserole.

- ❖ **1 whole rabbit**
- ❖ **Olive oil, for frying**
- ❖ **Sprigs of thyme**
- ❖ **Leeks, 2 large or 6 small, sliced**
- ❖ **Bulb of fennel, quartered and sliced**
- ❖ **250ml (8fl oz) ale**
- ❖ **1 head of garlic, broken into cloves**
- ❖ **1 apple, cored and roughly chopped**
- ❖ **Salt and freshly ground black pepper**

Preheat the oven to 180°C/350°F/gas 4.

Cook the rabbit in a large casserole with the oil over medium-high heat for 8 minutes per side, until golden brown. When you turn it over, stuff the thyme sprigs into the cavity.

Once the rabbit is browned, add the leeks, fennel, ale and garlic cloves into the pot with the rabbit and season to taste. Place in the oven, tightly covered, and cook for 1½ hours. After 45 minutes turn the rabbit over and add the apples.

Royal Beef Stew

For most Anglo-Saxons meat was scarce and used mainly as scraps for flavouring dishes. If meat was served, it would have been washed in water then soaked for possibly 12–48 hours, before being boiled in a cauldron over an open fire in the centre of the living space, which was usually a single room. Stewing for a long time made tough meat palatable and retained the nutrients in the cooking liquid.

Today there is no need to wash, soak and boil meat to make a stew, but to impart some Saxon character you can add vinegar, honey, leeks, celery and fennel. You can even add apricots, if you like. A stew this savoury would have required wealth.

Serves 6
- ❖ 2 tablespoons butter or chicken, pork or beef fat
- ❖ 1.1kg (2½lb) beef chuck or round, cut into 4–5cm (1½–2in) cubes
- ❖ 4 large leeks, white part only, roughly chopped
- ❖ 350g (12oz) carrots, peeled and cut into chunks
- ❖ 1 fennel bulb, trimmed and roughly chopped
- ❖ 3 celery stalks, roughly chopped
- ❖ 60ml (2½fl oz) vinegar
- ❖ 1 heaped tablespoon honey
- ❖ 1 bottle of red wine
- ❖ 1 heaped teaspoon black peppercorns
- ❖ 12 cloves
- ❖ Sprig of bay leaves
- ❖ 1 teaspoon salt
- ❖ A handful of sautéed chanterelles or morels, if available, added before serving

Heat the fat in a casserole pot over high heat and sear the beef pieces. Once browned all over, remove the meat to a platter.

Sauté the leeks, carrots, fennel and celery in the same pot until soft, about 10 minutes. Deglaze the pot with the vinegar and add in the honey.

Return the meat to the pot and pour in the wine to cover the meat and add the pepper and cloves. Place the bay sprig on top. Bring the stew to a boil, then immediately turn down the heat to a simmer. Cover and cook on low heat for 4 hours. Alternatively, cook in an oven set to 120°C/250°F/gas ½ for 4 hours.

Remove the fat, onion and celery, then reheat and taste for salt and pepper. The stew tastes best if it is cooled and kept overnight in the fridge.

Sauté the chanterelles or morels, if using, and add to the stew before serving with a thick slice of bread that's been toasted over the fire.

Brisket Hash

Hash is leftover meat that is chopped and cooked again with seasonings and onions. Often the hash is so good that brisket is made just to turn it into hash! Properly seasoned, it will not even need extra salt and pepper. Delicious served topped with fried or poached eggs, or with scrambled eggs and King Alfred's Cakes (see page 66).

❖ **390g (14oz) turnips, peeled and cut into 5mm (¼in) cubes**
❖ **Beef or chicken fat or olive oil, for frying**
❖ **1 onion, finely chopped**
❖ **4 handfuls of beef brisket (see page 118), cut into 5mm (¼in) cubes**
❖ **2 garlic cloves, minced**
❖ **1 tablespoon chopped fresh thyme**
❖ **150ml (150fl oz) double cream**
❖ **Salt and freshly ground black pepper**

Cook the turnips in a pan with the fat until crispy and brown on one side. Add the onion, then continue to cook until both the turnips and onion are brown. Add the beef, garlic and half the thyme and cook for 5 more minutes, stirring occasionally.

Pour in the cream and stir to combine, then press down on the hash with a spatula for 10–12 minutes until crispy and browned. Halfway through cooking, turn the hash over with the spatula. Sprinkle with the rest of the thyme. If needed, season with salt and pepper. Serve with your preferred topping.

Braised Lamb Shank

Around 1,000 years ago, like today, lamb shanks were
flavourful, economical and enhanced by longer cooking,
which gives texture to the braising liquid. This recipe includes
anchovies, which the Romans may have introduced, but other
preserved fish may be used, which the Anglo-Saxons would
have had in abundance. Soaking the anchovies makes them
softer so they melt into the base of the braise; it also draws out
salt, in case the cook should be salt mindful. The combination
of meat and fish provides an earthy, briny boost of umami,
enhanced here with the addition of mushrooms.

- 15g (½oz) of your favourite dried mushrooms,
  or 150g (5oz) sliced fresh mushrooms
- 2 lamb shanks
- 1 heaped tablespoon butter or chicken, pork or
  beef fat
- 1 onion, roughly chopped
- 2 garlic cloves, roughly chopped
- 2 anchovies, soaked and rinsed twice, chopped
- 120ml (4fl oz) raw apple cider vinegar
- 1 tablespoon fresh thyme leaves or 1 teaspoon dried
- 25g (1oz) fresh mint leaves, torn, or 2 tablespoons
  dried
- 1 tablespoon dried savory
- 8 small or 4 large carrots, cut into chunks, tops
  reserved
- 675g (1½lb) turnips, cut into chunks
- Salt and freshly ground black pepper

To dry mushrooms: put by the heat (125–150°C) for a day and leave to air dry for at least another three days.

Place the dried mushrooms in a small pot with enough water to cover, bring to a boil, then remove from the heat. Leave to steep for 30 minutes. Remove the mushrooms, drain (reserving the soaking liquid) and roughly chop. If using fresh mushrooms, rinse, slice and set aside.

Salt the shanks well, all around, rubbing the salt in a bit. Add the fat to a heavy-based pan and heat, then add the shanks and fry until browned. If you happen to have a good bed of coals in your hearth, place the shanks on the grate and rotate until browned. You can also grill them, depending on the flavours you desire most.

Preheat the oven to 200°C/400°F/gas 6.

Set a large casserole over medium heat and when hot spoon in your fat (if butter, let it start to brown) and add in the onion and garlic and a pinch of salt and stir together, cooking and stirring every minute or so until translucent, about 3 minutes. Stir in the anchovies, mashing them with a wooden spoon, and cook until the onions are lightly browned along the edges, but not burned – 3 more minutes. Deglaze the pan with the vinegar, stirring for 1 minute to remove any brown bits from the base of the pan. Add all the herbs, chopped carrot tops and pepper and stir for 1 minute, then add in the mushrooms and their soaking liquid (if using dried mushrooms).

Settle in the browned shanks at the bottom of the pot, nestled into the braising base. Add in enough water to cover the shanks by three-quarters. Layer the turnips and carrots on top, mixing the two. Bring to a hard boil, then cover with a lid and transfer to the oven to cook for 3 hours. After this time, remove the lid and return to the oven for 15 minutes, to brown the vegetables and reduce the liquid.

To serve, set a shank into a large bowl and top with the turnip and carrot mix, spooning over the braising sauce.

Spatchcocked Chicken

This playful presentation arises from the 'blood eagle' execution famed in Norse sagas. In truth, it is a foolproof method of roasting the perfect chicken; it opens the cavity, which allows for even and immediate heat distribution, whether the chicken is grilled, smoked or barbecued.

- ❖ 1 chicken (free-range or organic)
- ❖ 1 tablespoon Saxon rub (see page 221)
- ❖ Sea salt

Preheat the oven to 220°C/425°F/gas 7.

First things first, spatchcock the bird! Simply insert your kitchen shears and cut along the backbone, starting up from the tail and going all the way up to the neck. Cut up along one side, then the other. Reserve this backbone, as it contains all the necessaries for making a simple chicken stock (see page 123). (You can also simply place it below the bird and roast it before adding to stock.) Crack open or break the breastbone by flattening the chicken down with your hands – apply equal pressure so as not to bruise the flesh. If you prefer, you can ask the butcher to do this for you.

Next, season the bird. Salt it front and back, and all around, then apply your rub, sprinkling it over liberally to provide a good covering.

Place the chicken breast side up in a deep roasting pan, which will do a fantastic job of collecting any rendered fat for you to use in other applications, or to dip the meat into, or baste as it nears completion, if you like.

Place in the oven and roast for 45–50 minutes, or until the bird reaches an internal temperature of 75°C (165°F). You can opt to drop the oven temperature to around 110°C/225°F/ gas ¼ or so after the first 10 minutes, to allow the bird to 'slow cook'; if you do this, allow 1 hour 30 minutes to 2 hours to cook, depending on the size of your bird.

Meatballs from Three Animals

Using knives and axes, the Saxons chopped and minced meat and cut small portions of joints for meatballs, sausages and puddings. The minced mixtures could be made from any edible animal or bird. This recipe uses three meats: lamb, pork and beef. The combination, including the fat from the lamb and pork, creates delicious meatballs with excellent flavour and texture. We add mint, which was available to the Saxons, but if you prefer you can use finely chopped thyme, chives or sage – the Saxons thought these herbs had substantial healing powers. Another great combination is 60% pork and 40% venison, which would have been an option for the Saxon nobility.

For this recipe we have smothered the meatballs in a rich creamy gravy, which is a modern way of serving them.

Makes about 50 meatballs
- ❖ **2 tablespoons fat or olive oil**
- ❖ **1 large onion, chopped**
- ❖ **50g (2oz) fine breadcrumbs**
- ❖ **120ml (4fl oz) double cream or almond milk**
- ❖ **1 teaspoon minced garlic**
- ❖ **450g (1lb) minced beef**
- ❖ **450g (1lb) minced pork shoulder**
- ❖ **450g (1lb) minced lamb – preferably shoulder**
- ❖ **1 large egg**
- ❖ **1 tablespoon honey**
- ❖ **3 tablespoons chopped parsley**
- ❖ **2 tablespoons chopped fresh mint**
- ❖ **Salt and freshly ground black pepper**

For the sauce
- ❖ **500ml (18fl oz) chicken stock, bought or homemade (see page 123)**
- ❖ **240ml (8fl oz) double cream**
- ❖ **1 tablespoon lingonberry jam**
- ❖ **3–4 tablespoons juice from the pickles**

Preheat the oven to 180°C/350°F/gas 4.

Warm the fat in a large pan over medium heat, and cook the minced garlic and onion for 5 minutes, until softened, then set aside to cool.

Combine the breadcrumbs and 120ml (4fl oz) cream or milk in a bowl and set aside for about 5 minutes to absorb the liquid and soften.

In a large mixing bowl combine the beef, pork, lamb, onion, garlic, egg, honey, parsley and mint. Season liberally with salt and pepper. Add the bread and cream mixture and stir well, then form into meatballs. Place the meatballs on a baking sheet lined with tin foil. Bake in the oven for 20 minutes.

Meanwhile, prepare the sauce. In a large frying pan, whisk together the stock, 120ml (4fl oz) cream, jam and pickle juice and bring to a simmer. Season to taste with salt and pepper.

Add the cooked meatballs to the sauce, reduce the heat to medium, and simmer for about 5 minutes, until the sauce thickens slightly and the meatballs are heated through.

Grilled Liver

Liver is a relatively inexpensive ingredient that has a gamey, unique taste. The quality of the liver used for this recipe is key, though, so get the best you can. Livers of large animals like pigs and cows benefit from marinating before grilling, while those from small animals like chickens and rabbits may not need a marinade.

* ❖ 1 liver (calf or pork is preferred, but beef is very good, just stronger!)
* ❖ Lard or good-quality olive oil
* ❖ 1 tablespoon salt and freshly ground black pepper
* ❖ 3 tablespoons fresh herbs, such as mint, rosemary, dill, or Saxon rub (see page 221)
* ❖ Apple cider vinegar, to serve (optional)

Rinse the liver, and if an outer membrane is attached, pull it away with your fingers. Slice the liver into pieces about 1cm (½in) thick and place in a baking dish in one layer. Rub the slices with the lard or oil and sprinkle with salt and pepper, then sprinkle over some chopped fresh herbs or Saxon rub. Set aside in the fridge, covered, for about an hour, or overnight if you really want the flavours to penetrate. Bring the slices to room temperature prior to grilling.

Grill about 10cm (4in) above coals or below the grill, about 3 minutes a side – the timing depends on the size of the liver. You want the liver to still be pink in the middle; since it is lean, it can toughen with extended cooking. If you prefer, cook in a frying pan over medium-high heat. Taste a little before serving – if it's a bit too rich, pour over a splash of apple cider vinegar.

Juniper-spiced Boar Meatballs

To the Saxons the wild boar was a symbol of strength and fertility, and its image adorned helmets and was used on battle banners. A feast featuring boar meat showcased a lord's power and built camaraderie, because boar was not accessible to the lower classes.

Juniper berries have a distinct flavour, intense aroma and soft heat. The berries are lightly crushed before use as a spice, and are still used today to season game, pork, cabbage and sauerkraut.

Makes 30 bite-sized meatballs
- ❖ **2 teaspoons olive oil, plus extra for frying**
- ❖ **1 small onion, chopped**
- ❖ **2 teaspoons lightly crushed juniper berries**
- ❖ **450g (1lb) minced boar**
- ❖ **1 egg**
- ❖ **25g (1oz) breadcrumbs**
- ❖ **Salt and freshly ground black pepper**

Warm the olive oil in a frying pan over medium heat and cook the onion for 5 minutes, until softened. Add the crushed juniper berries, stirring to let the onions absorb the juniper. Take off the heat and leave to cool.

In a bowl, combine the boar, cooled onion, egg and breadcrumbs. Season liberally with salt and pepper and form into meatballs.

Cook the meatballs in a little oil in a large frying pan until crispy on the outside and cooked through, about 10 minutes.

Pluck Hash

(the leftover goodies put to use)

Birds and rabbits provide little gifts that often go unused. This hash has a strong meat flavour, making it suitable for many uses. You can buy the meat pieces at farmers' markets or from the butcher – always ask for free-range or organic if you can. A healthy growing environment produces better animal organs.

Liver is a good source of iron and has a gamey flavour, which you should try to embrace. Gizzards should be cooked for long periods to make them tender, but should be chopped well for this dish. Rabbit kidneys are mild and tender, while hearts taste like the meat of the animal.

Eat the hash atop barley or porridge, within a pottage or with scrambled eggs. You can add griddled onions to make a delicious sandwich.

- ❖ **Preferred fat, for frying**
- ❖ **Chicken and/or rabbit hearts and livers**
- ❖ **Chicken gizzards**
- ❖ **Rabbit kidneys**
- ❖ **Ale (optional)**
- ❖ **Salt and freshly ground black pepper**

Chop all the ingredients well.

Pour the fat into a non-stick frying pan over medium-high heat. Add the meat to the pan, season with salt and pepper, and stir occasionally, allowing bits to crisp up and cook through. This can be cooked quickly, or you can let it go low and slow to tenderise, maybe adding a little ale to deglaze the pan or even braise it.

Quail for Court

Quail and other game from hunting and fowling was food for the wealthy and suitable for feasts. Preparing feast foods took considerable skill, and quail is a delicacy that's still suitable for modern-day feasts. The key is to cook the quail quickly to keep the juices inside.

Pan-braised Quail

Pan-braising involves browning the meat, then simmering it in liquid, which keeps the quail from drying out and also creates a flavourful gravy. In the second recipe we have called for tea and vinegar for the liquid, but feel free to substitute it with red wine if you prefer. Saxon lords had access to both.

- ❖ 6 quail
- ❖ 1 heaped tablespoon chicken fat or olive oil
- ❖ Pinch of fresh chopped thyme
- ❖ 175ml (6fl oz) red wine
- ❖ 1 tablespoon double cream
- ❖ 5 tablespoons butter
- ❖ Salt and freshly ground black pepper

Sear the quail in a pan over high heat with the fat until browned. Sprinkle the birds with the thyme, salt and pepper. Cook each side until brown, about 8 minutes in total. Remove the quail to a plate.

Pour the red wine into the same pan and reduce the liquid until the surface is covered with bubbles. The sauce will reduce to about 60ml (2½fl oz). Add the cream and whisk together. Then add the butter, one tablespoon after the other, swirling the pan or whisking it all together. Put the quail back in the pan over low heat and turn every few minutes over about 10 minutes.

To serve, pour the sauce over the quail.

Quail Braised in Vinegar and Tea

- ❖ 6 quail
- ❖ 2–3 pears, cored and cut into chunks (or other stone fruit)
- ❖ 1 tablespoon chicken fat or olive oil
- ❖ Handful of fresh sage leaves
- ❖ 175ml (6fl oz) freshly brewed tea
- ❖ 1 tablespoon cider vinegar, or to taste
- ❖ 1 teaspoon honey
- ❖ 5 tablespoons butter
- ❖ Salt and freshly ground black pepper

Sear the quail and pears in a hot frying pan over high heat with the fat. Add the sage leaves, salt and pepper. Cook each side until brown, for a total of 8 minutes. Remove the quail to a plate.

Pour the tea, vinegar and honey into a pan over medium heat and reduce the liquid until the surface is covered with bubbles. The sauce will reduce to about 60ml (2½fl oz). Add the butter, one tablespoon after the other, swirling the pan or whisking it all together. Put the quail back in the pan over low heat and turn every few minutes over about 10 minutes.

Braised Beef Brisket

Brisket is cut from the breast or lower chest of a cow or calf. These muscles support a lot of weight so the meat is full of connective tissue, which can be tenderised by slow cooking. The meat can be smoked, roasted or boiled, as long as it is done slowly. Brisket leftovers can be used to make amazing hash or sandwiches with sauerkraut (see pages 104 and 212).

- ❖ Beef brisket (about 1.3kg/3lb)
- ❖ Vegetable oil, for frying
- ❖ 900g (2lb) yellow onions, halved, quartered or sliced
- ❖ 1 head garlic, sliced in half, or a few garlic cloves, minced
- ❖ 2–3 carrots, peeled and chopped
- ❖ 2–3 celery stalks, chopped
- ❖ A few bay leaves
- ❖ A few sprigs of thyme
- ❖ 500ml (18fl oz) chicken stock, bought or homemade (see page 123)
- ❖ 500–750ml (18fl oz–1¼ pints) red wine
- ❖ 1 tablespoon cider vinegar
- ❖ Coarse salt and freshly ground black pepper

Preheat the oven to 150°C/300°F/gas 2.

Pat the brisket dry with kitchen paper and season with salt and pepper.

Add the oil to a casserole pot over medium-high heat. When the oil is very hot, sear the brisket on all sides, 3–6 minutes each side, and place the meat on a plate.

Add the onions, garlic, carrots, celery and herbs to the pot and brown the vegetables, scraping the browned bits at the bottom for a couple of minutes. Add the stock and wine, bring to a boil, then turn the heat off. Add the brisket, tucking it into the vegetables, and put on the lid. Transfer to the oven and cook for 2½ hours. To test if the meat is done, plunge a fork into the brisket – you want the meat to give, but not shred. For melt-in-your-mouth brisket, after 3–3½ hours, it should be falling apart easily.

To eat immediately, let the brisket cool enough to handle, then slice against the grain – this breaks down the muscle fibres, which makes the meat melty tender. Braised brisket is easier to slice when chilled and tastes better when reheated the next day, because the flavours meld together overnight.

To serve up to 3 days later, store it in the fridge submerged in the cooking liquid. To reheat, slice while cold, against the grain, then arrange the slices in a baking dish and cover with the cooking liquid. Cover tightly and reheat in the oven at 120°C/250°F/gas ½ for 45 minutes.

Venison Stew

Deer were raised in enclosed parks to provide food for the wealthy, while the peasants would have to poach the animals if they wanted to eat venison, unless they had a favoured position with the local lord or lady. The stag (male deer) was considered the best meat.

Venison has absolutely no fat, so it becomes dry when roasted. Instead, use a haunch of venison to make this superb stew. You can make the rich sauce from venison stock using tough and stringy bits of leftovers, red wine, onions and carrots. You can also add a bit of gin for flavour – although of course the Saxons would not have been able to do that – and add breadcrumbs to thicken the stew.

The marinade can be made from whatever combination of vegetables and spices you have to hand, but I've given a suggestion for ingredients here.

Serves 8
- ❖ **1.8–2.25kg (4–5lb) venison from the haunch, cut into 5cm (2in) chunks**

For the marinade
- ❖ **1 onion**
- ❖ **A couple of carrots and celery stalks**
- ❖ **1–2 garlic cloves**
- ❖ **1–2 shallots**
- ❖ **Handful of juniper berries**
- ❖ **2–3 cloves**
- ❖ **1 teaspoon allspice**

❖ **1–2 sprigs of rosemary, thyme or bay leaves**
❖ **Splash of red wine**
❖ **Salt and freshly ground black pepper**

For the stew
❖ **4–5 slices of bacon**
❖ **Butter and olive oil, for frying**
❖ **Splash of gin, for frying**
❖ **Homemade venison or other meat stock (see page 123)**
❖ **About 375ml (13fl oz) red wine**
❖ **2–3 sprigs of thyme, tied together**
❖ **1 small white onion, blanched and peeled**
❖ **A few carrots, peeled and roughly chopped**
❖ **A few parsnips, peeled and roughly cut**
❖ **Handful of fresh breadcrumbs**
❖ **Handful of sliced mushrooms and frozen peas (optional)**

First marinate the meat. Combine the meat with the vegetables in a large pot and cover with wine, then put it in the fridge overnight.

When you are ready to cook the meat drain and reserve the marinade. Dry the meat thoroughly with kitchen paper.

Preheat the oven to 150°C/300°F/gas 2.

Fry the bacon until crispy, then cut into small pieces and set aside. Mix the fat in the pan from the bacon with some butter and olive oil. Season the venison and cook in the pan, browning the meat on all sides, adding more butter if you need to throughout.

Heat a small amount of gin in a saucepan and use it to briefly flambé the browned meat in the pan to seal in the juice. Put out the flame with a large pan lid.

Take the reserved, strained marinade and with equal parts of marinade, venison stock and red wine, combine the meat and liquid with the bacon in an ovenproof casserole. Bring to a boil, then lower the heat to a simmer and add the fresh thyme sprigs. Transfer the stew to the oven and cook for around 3 hours, until tender – slow cooking works best.

Add the vegetables in the last 90 minutes of cooking – depending on how tender the meat is. If you cannot tell how long the stew needs, then sauté the baby onions, carrots and parsnips in a little oil over high heat until very slightly caramelised, then add to the stew when the meat is tender and comes out of the oven. When the meat and vegetables are tender, thicken the sauce on the hob by adding the breadcrumbs.

Before serving add some mushrooms and peas to brighten up the stew, if you like. Remove the bay leaves and herbs before serving.

Stocks

When cooking meat, reserve any bones to make stock that you can use to enhance the flavour or other dishes. Leftover bones from a picked-over bird, or pork, lamb or beef work wonderfully, but many butchers can provide chicken backs, pigs' feet, beef soup bones, etc., if you ask for them.

Roasting the bones before making the stock will add extra flavour, but you can make a good stock by just boiling the bones long and slow. Technique snobs might howl, but with this long and harder method of making stock you will not need to worry about straining and skimming the liquid. This recipe will use anything that the bones and untrimmed bits offer, wonderfully emulsifying them into liquid gold, with a full-bodied texture rich in vitamins and full of collagen.

If adding vegetables to the base, do not do so until the final half hour to 45 minutes, otherwise your stock will be full of vegetable mush. Stocks freeze and keep very well – so stock up!

* **Bones and meat trimmings**
* **Pinch of salt**

Place the bones and trimmings into a large pot and enough water to cover the bones by about 3cm (1¼in). Add a pinch of salt. Bring to a boil that's just above a simmer – not too fierce, with just gentle bubbles – and keep covered, then cook over low heat for 12 hours. Check the stock occasionally, adding more water if it looks like it is reducing too much.

Vegetable Stock Variation

The Saxons would have had meat-based stocks, soups and broths, leaving teas and elixirs as the purely vegetal option, but this recipe is for those desiring a meat-free version. For this stock you can roast the vegetables first or use roasted leftovers, if you like, or add them uncooked, which means the overall cooking time will be far less.

* Leftover or fresh vegetables and trimmings, roughly chopped
* Pinch of salt
* Pinch of your favourite fresh herbs

Place the vegetables in a large pot, cover with water, add a pinch of salt and your preferred herbs, then bring to a rolling boil before turning the heat down and simmering for 30–45 minutes.

WILD VEGETABLES

Cream-braised Leeks with Nutmeg

Leeks were the most popular vegetable eaten by the Saxons, and as they liked to spice their food with dill, poppy, caraway, fennel and sweet cicely seeds, we've added these seeds to creamed leeks. This also makes a good filling for an omelette.

- ❖ **1–2 tablespoons butter**
- ❖ **3 small leeks, white and light green part roughly chopped**
- ❖ **1 tablespoon single cream**
- ❖ **Freshly grated nutmeg, to taste**
- ❖ **Salt and freshly ground black pepper**

Melt the butter in a frying pan over medium-high heat. Throw in the leeks and leave alone until they start getting a bit charred. Stir, then pour in the cream. Stir for a moment or two, until the cream has thickened and almost disappeared. Add some nutmeg, salt and grindings of pepper. Serve right away.

Beetroots

Beetroots are old, and even by 300 BC there were many varieties. Beets have a high sugar content and need to be cooked until they are tender but not mushy.

When preparing the beetroots, do not throw the leaves away! Try sautéing the greens with a chopped onion, then throw in mint leaves, currants and garlic. The Saxons had all these ingredients and they might have cooked beetroot greens in this manner.

Lightly Pickled Beetroots

These are very good with salty meats.

- ❖ **Bunch of small beetroots (about 15–20)**
- ❖ **60ml (2½fl oz) vinegar**
- ❖ **1 tablespoon honey**
- ❖ **1 bay leaf**

Cut off the stems and cook the beetroots in simmering water for 15 minutes or until a sharp knife tip easily pierces the beetroot. Leave to cool, then peel.

Put the vinegar, honey and bay leaf in a saucepan, bring to a boil and simmer for a few minutes. Pour this hot brine over the peeled beetroots.

Transfer to clean jars, seal tightly and store in a cold spot.

Roasted Beetroots

❖ **Beetroots**

Preheat the oven to 200°C/400°F/gas 6.

Remove the top of the beetroot stem, leaving a 1cm (½in) stem. Wash the beetroots and place them in a baking tray with a little water. Cover with foil and roast until easily pierced with a knife tip – depending on their size, this should take 45 minutes to 1 hour. Leave to cool, then peel.

Braised Greens

These greens are a mix of foraged and cultivated vegetables. A quick note here: you will want to be certain of the soil health of any greens that you forage, as many, especially dandelion, have a very good habit of drawing in highly toxic heavy metals whenever they are present in the soil. Unspoiled locations are best, and if you live in the city, contact the local authorities for guidance. Colleges and universities will test soil samples as well.

Using herbs is optional; mint is a great herb for many, many reasons, but it is a wonderful addition in savoury dishes. When cooked long and slow, the typical flavour draws down and becomes mild but soothing.

- ❖ **Mixed and foraged (or foraged 'themed') greens, as available, such as dandelions, mustard leaves, kale, turnip or carrot tops, romaine lettuce, Swiss chard**
- ❖ **1 garlic clove, sliced**
- ❖ **Herbs, such as mint, lemon balm, dill, thyme or savory (mix as you like, or focus on one flavour, or none at all)**
- ❖ **Salt, to taste**

Clean the greens. Rinse thoroughly – nothing cleanses better than a bucket and a couple of fills of water, particularly for root vegetable greens, or anything that branches up through the ground as it grows. A bowl or sink are all great, but I do like washing them with the garden hose and a bucket!

Cut all greens to the sizes that you prefer and place in a large pot. Throw in the sliced garlic and the herbs, if you are using them. Fill the pot with water no higher than halfway up to the top of the greens, as the greens will collapse into the water as they cook down. Cook until done.

Eat as a side, or as a salad, tossed with green sauce (see page 133).

Fennel

Bitter fennel (the original wild fennel) was cultivated by the Egyptians and used as early as 3000 BC as a medicinal herb. Fennel was prized by the ancient Greeks and Romans as a medicine, a vegetable, a flavouring and as an insect repellent. Warriors believed fennel tea gave them courage before battle. Fennel is one of the nine plants invoked in the pagan Anglo-Saxon *Nine Herbs Charm*, recorded in the tenth century. Saxon farmers grew many vegetables around their houses, including carrots, parsnip, cabbages, peas, beans, onions and fennel.

Fennel bulbs should be heavy for their size, with no brown spots. The feathery fronds should show no signs of wilting.

Braised Fennel

- ❖ **2 large fennel bulbs, with fronds**
- ❖ **1 tablespoon fat**
- ❖ **2 teaspoons fennel seeds**
- ❖ **Salt and freshly ground black pepper**

Trim the fennel, reserving the fronds, and cut the bulbs into eighths. Put the fennel wedges in a saucepan with the fat and 175ml (6fl oz) water and stew over medium heat for 5 minutes, covered.

Sprinkle the fennel with the fennel seeds, salt and pepper. Turn the fennel over, raise the heat and cook for about 10 minutes more, until the liquid has evaporated and the fennel is cooked through and caramelised.

Roasted Fennel

- ❖ **2 large fennel bulbs, with fronds**
- ❖ **1 tablespoon olive oil**
- ❖ **Pinch of fennel seeds**
- ❖ **Salt and freshly ground black pepper**

Preheat the oven to 220°C/425°F/gas 7.

Cut the fennel bulbs into quarters, reserving the fronds. Toss the bulbs in the olive oil in a baking tin, then cook in the oven for 1¼ hours.

To serve, sprinkle the crispy roast fennel with salt and pepper, the reserved fennel fronds and a pinch of fennel seeds.

Dandelion Salad with Bacon

Dandelions are bitter, chewy and full of vitamins. Warm bacon fat creates a delicious blend with the bitterness of dandelion greens.

- ❖ **115g (4oz) thick-cut bacon from the belly, cut into cubes**
- ❖ **Bunch of dandelions, washed, dried, thick stems removed and leaves torn**
- ❖ **1 tablespoon cider vinegar**
- ❖ **1 tablespoon Dijon mustard**
- ❖ **Salt and freshly ground black pepper**

Fry the bacon over low-medium heat until almost crispy – some bits really crispy and some not at all is a great combo. Drain the bacon on a piece of kitchen paper, reserving the fat.

Put the dandelion leaves and bacon cubes into a salad bowl.

Measure out 3 tablespoons of the bacon fat and discard the rest. Pour the fat back into the pan and warm through. Whisk the vinegar and mustard into the hot fat, then add salt and pepper to taste.

Pour the dressing over the salad and serve right away.

A Green Sauce

Many herbs, both wild and cultivated, were used in Anglo-Saxon tonics and foods. This is an excellent sauce for grilled and roasted meat or fish and makes a good topping for the common turnip. A spoonful will enhance the taste of barley pottage.

You may make this as you like, focusing on what is readily available and plentiful. During the colder months, use dried varieties, perhaps heating them over low heat to extract flavours, or leaving them to sit at room temperature for many hours. The saltiness of the anchovies negates the need for any additional salt.

- **Bunch each of fresh mint, dill, thyme sprigs and chives**
- **Bunch of carrot tops**
- **Anchovies, to taste**
- **Apple cider vinegar, to loosen**
- **Lard, chicken fat or tallow, or melted butter (for fattier meats, you may not need to add animal fat)**
- **Freshly ground pepper, to taste**

Finely chop all the herbs and the carrot tops, and depending on the desired texture also grind them using a mortar and pestle. Finely chop in the anchovies, and again grind if you like. Pour in enough cider vinegar to get the sauce to your desired consistency, mixing in some fat as desired. Add some pepper to taste.

Foraged Mushroom Omelette

Since we know the Saxons made omelettes, it is easy to imagine them doing so with foraged mushrooms. Mushrooms reduce greatly when sautéed, so use more here than you might think is necessary. You can fold the omelette to fit our modern plates, or invert it onto a plate.

Serves 1
- ❖ **A few mushrooms, oyster, shiitake, chanterelles, morels or even crimini, wiped clean, woody stems removed, thickly sliced**
- ❖ **2 tablespoons unsalted butter**
- ❖ **2 eggs, at room temperature**
- ❖ **Salt and freshly ground black pepper**

Put the sliced mushrooms and 1 tablespoon of the butter in a small pan over medium-high heat and sauté until the mushrooms are slightly browned and have released their liquid.

While the mushrooms are cooking, crack the eggs into a bowl and beat lightly.

Add the rest of the butter to the pan and pour the eggs over the foaming butter and mushrooms. Leave for 30 seconds, then use a fork to pull the edges of the omelette into the centre of the pan, letting the uncooked egg fill in the gaps. Repeat all around the sides. When the surface is set but still soft, invert the omelette onto a plate. Sprinkle with a pinch of salt and a few grinds of black pepper.

Sage and Pepper Omelette

Both sage and pepper were used in cooking by the Romans –
sage for its medicinal qualities, too – and there are references
to both in Saxon writings.

Sage, eggs, salt and pepper; simple, delicious and perfect for a
Sunday morning.

Serves 1
- ❖ **2 eggs, at room temperature**
- ❖ **1 heaped tablespoon of finely chopped sage leaves,
  plus some for garnish**
- ❖ **½ teaspoon freshly ground pepper, or to taste**
- ❖ **1 tablespoon unsalted butter**
- ❖ **Salt, to taste**

Crack the eggs into a bowl and beat lightly. Whisk the sage
and pepper into the egg mixture.

Melt the butter in a small frying pan, and when it is sizzling
pour the eggs over the foaming butter. Leave for 30 seconds,
then use a fork to pull the edges of the omelette into the
centre of the pan, letting the uncooked egg fill in the gaps.
Repeat all around the sides. When the surface is set but still
soft, invert the omelette onto a plate. Sprinkle with a good
pinch of salt, some more chopped sage leaves and a few
grinds of black pepper.

Chanterelle Toast

This dish is a tasty, easy treat.

- ❖ **450g (1lb) chanterelles**
- ❖ **Thick slices of bread**
- ❖ **Double cream, to serve**
- ❖ **Salt and freshly ground black pepper**

Preheat the oven to 220°C/425°F/gas 7.

Clean the chanterelles and lay them on a baking sheet. Cook in the oven until browned, about 45 minutes. They will shrink a lot, since mushrooms contain so much water.

Meanwhile, toast or grill thick slices of excellent bread.

Toss the roasted mushrooms with a bit of heavy cream and salt and freshly ground pepper. Spoon onto the toast and serve.

WATER

Grilled Trout

Simple and fresh. Nothing says dinner in northern lands like campfire grilled trout. You can roast this fish, cook it over a wood fire or pan-fry it. We aren't looking to fill the trout with vegetables, but to flavour it as it cooks, so use herbs that are fresh and available to you – the list below is a good starting point.

- ❖ **Whole trout, preferably head on and butterflied**
- ❖ **Lard, for greasing**
- ❖ **Herbs, such as dill, fennel fronds, chives, lemon balm, mint**
- ❖ **Kitchen string**
- ❖ **Salt and freshly ground black pepper**

Rinse the trout and pat dry with kitchen paper. Rub all over with the lard and season with salt and pepper, inside and out. Place a few of the herbs so that the fish will have contact with the herbs as it cooks. Tie in place with the string.

If roasting in the oven, preheat it to 180°C/350°F/gas 4 and cook for about 25 minutes. If you are pan-frying the fish, place in a frying pan over medium-high heat, cooking for 4–6 minutes on each side. If you are cooking over coals, cook for about 5 minutes for each side, either on the grate or wrap the fish in a sheet of tin foil and place the parcel among the coals, for about 7–8 minutes.

Eel Pie

This is a classic pie, using what well-to-do Saxons had: raisins, figs and almond milk.

For the pastry
- ❖ 75g (3oz) butter, cold
- ❖ 75g (3oz) lard, cold
- ❖ 250g (9oz) flour, plus extra for dusting
- ❖ 4–5 tablespoons iced water

For the filling
- ❖ 450g (1lb) eel, skinned, boned and cut into bite-sized pieces
- ❖ 240ml (8fl oz) fish stock
- ❖ ½ teaspoon ground ginger
- ❖ ¼ teaspoon ground cinnamon
- ❖ 240ml (8fl oz) almond milk
- ❖ 1 turnip, roughly diced
- ❖ 1 celery stalk, sliced
- ❖ 1 carrot, roughly diced
- ❖ 1 leek, sliced
- ❖ 75g (3oz) raisins, mashed
- ❖ 65g (2½oz) dried figs, chopped
- ❖ Salt and freshly ground black pepper

Cut the cold fats into the flour in a mixing bowl with two knives, a blender or your fingers. When crumbly add 4 tablespoons of the iced water. Mix the dough into a ball, adding another tablespoon of water if needed. Set aside in the fridge while you cook the filling.

Cook the eel in the fish stock until almost tender, then season with salt, pepper, ginger and cinnamon. Remove the eel chunks and set aside.

Add the almond milk to the pan of stock and cook the turnips, celery, carrot and leek until almost tender, about 10 minutes. Drain.

Preheat the oven to 170°C/325°F/gas 3. Meanwhile, divide the dough into two and roll out one piece on a work surface dusted with flour until large enough to line an ovenproof casserole. Roll out the other piece to the size of a pastry lid.

Add the eel to the pastry-lined casserole, then scatter the fruits over the top. Cover with the pastry lid, pressing the edge down all the way round to seal it. Transfer to the oven and bake for 1 hour.

Pickled Herring

Herring is a little bony fish; fresh herring does not keep long so it is usually preserved in salt, pickled or smoked.

This recipe uses two brines; the salt in the first brine takes out extra moisture from the fish and keeps the flesh firm. Do not skip the first brine or the herring will turn to mush. If you use pre-salted herring from a can, soak the fish in fresh water overnight and skip the first brine, the herring will be firm and salty enough.

For the first brine
- 1 litre (1¾ pints) water
- 135g (4½oz) salt
- 450g (1lb) herring fillets

For the pickling brine
- 500ml (18fl oz) white vinegar
- 100g (3½oz) sugar
- 250ml (9fl oz) water
- 3 bay leaves
- 3 cloves
- 2 teaspoons black peppercorns
- 1 onion, sliced

Combine the water and salt in a large saucepan and bring to a boil to dissolve the salt. Pour into a heatproof bowl and leave to cool, then transfer to the fridge until chilled. Add the herring into the chilled brine, cover and leave in the fridge for 1–3 days.

After 2 days, make the pickling brine. Combine the vinegar, sugar, water, bay leaves, cloves and peppercorns. Bring to a boil, then lower the heat to a simmer and cook for 15 minutes. Pour into a bowl and place in the fridge until chilled.

Remove the herring from the first brine, layer them into glass jars with the sliced onion. Cover with the cold pickling brine and seal the jars. Wait for two days before eating. Store in a cold place for up to 1 month.

Kettle of Fish

'Brod' was the Old English term for broth, and Anglo-Saxon broth was a thin liquid; carrot and mint broths were mentioned in *Leechdoms*. For this recipe, carrot broth can be purchased in bottles.

Herring, salmon, cod, eel, pike and perch, smelt, halibut and welk bones have been recovered in early Anglo-Saxon settlements. If the Saxons made fish stews they probably threw in salted fish too. The point is that fish stew was made with what was available, both then and now, so this is a liberal interpretation to get a feeling of what might be caught and gathered and cooked in the pot on the fire.

For the broth
- ❖ **6 tablespoons unsalted butter**
- ❖ **50g (2oz) minced celery**
- ❖ **150g (5oz) minced shallots**
- ❖ **45g (2oz) diced fennel**
- ❖ **5 garlic cloves, minced**
- ❖ **Large bunch of thyme**
- ❖ **250ml (8fl oz) white wine**
- ❖ **250ml (8fl oz) carrot juice**
- ❖ **1 litre (1¾ pints) fish stock (or 2 bottles of clam juice)**
- ❖ **Salt and freshly ground black pepper**

For the seafood
- ❖ **4 tablespoons olive oil (or use lard or chicken fat)**
- ❖ **Mussels in their shells, scrubbed and de-bearded**
- ❖ **Shrimp, peeled and deveined**

❖ **Turbot, halibut and any other white fish, cut into
   bite-sized chunks**
❖ **2 shallots, chopped**

First make the broth. Melt 4 tablespoons of the butter
in a saucepan over medium heat until foamy. Stir in the
vegetables, herbs and 1 teaspoon each of salt and pepper
and cook until translucent, about 8–10 minutes.

Halfway through the cooking process, add the remaining
2 tablespoons of butter. Add the wine, carrot juice and fish
stock, stir together and bring to a boil. Turn off the heat and
put the lid on the pot to keep the sauce warm.

Season the seafood with salt and pepper. In a wide and deep
sauté pan, warm the olive oil, then add the mussels and cook
for 1–2 minutes, until they open. Add the shrimp, fish and
shallots and cook until opaque on one side, about 90 seconds.
Add the broth and stir, covering the pan to let the seafood
steam until cooked through, about 2–3 minutes. Just before
serving, remove any mussels whose shells have not opened.

Oyster Stew

An oyster stew would have been a feast day meal, as oysters were confined to the wealthy until the mid-seventeenth century. This stew showcases the treasures found in the forest and sea. The cream ties the mushrooms, oysters and herbs together, and the bread makes the perfect foundation. We can imagine people putting this stew together after foraging in the forest, after which the picked mushrooms would be threaded onto strings and hung up and dried for use as and when needed.

Serves 2
- ❖ **4 tablespoons butter**
- ❖ **2 thick slices of crusty bread**
- ❖ **12 oysters, shucked**
- ❖ **15g (½oz) dried mushrooms – chanterelles, porcinis, morels**
- ❖ **120ml (4fl oz) double cream**
- ❖ **Generous handful of sage leaves, finely chopped**
- ❖ **Generous handful of thyme, leaves picked**
- ❖ **Generous handful of snipped dill**
- ❖ **Salt and freshly ground black pepper**

Melt 2 tablespoons of the butter in a frying pan. Once melted, add the bread slices and fry, flipping once and cooking so that both sides are golden brown, about 4 minutes. Set aside.

Melt the remaining butter in a saucepan. Stir in the shucked oysters along with 120ml (4fl oz) of their liquor (substitute clam juice if you are short on oyster liquor). Cook, barely simmering, until the oysters plump up and begin to ruffle at their edges, about 4 minutes.

Add the mushrooms and pour in the cream. Stir and simmer gently until warmed through, about 3 minutes. Take care not to let the mixture boil. Sprinkle with the herbs, plenty of freshly ground pepper and sprinkling of salt.

Place a slice of fried bread in the bottom of a wide shallow bowl, then spoon over 6 oysters and pour half of the creamy broth over the top. Sprinkle with salt and pepper to taste. Repeat with the other slice of bread and the rest of the oysters and broth.

Haddock Simmered in Ale

This is fast-cooking, delicious and unusual. Be sure to use a pale ale so as not to overpower the clean taste of haddock. We can envision an Anglo-Saxon throwing a haddock on the fire and pouring a little ale in the pan! For an ancient riff on fish and chips, serve the haddock with parsnip chips (see page 50).

- ❖ 2 shallots, chopped
- ❖ 4 garlic cloves, minced
- ❖ 1 bottle of ale, on the paler side
- ❖ 675g (1½lb) haddock fillets
- ❖ 2 tablespoons butter (optional)
- ❖ Salt and freshly ground black pepper

In a deep frying pan large enough to hold the haddock in one layer, cook the shallots and garlic until softened, about 2–3 minutes.

Pour in the bottle of ale and bring to a low boil. Turn down the heat to a feisty simmer and add the haddock fillets. After 6 minutes, turn the haddock over and cook for a further 6 minutes. Depending on the thickness the fish should be perfectly cooked after this – the flesh will be flaky when a knife tip pierces the flesh.

Remove the fish to a plate. You can serve it alone, or create an opulent, more modern sauce by reducing the remaining ale over high heat, adding 2 tablespoons of butter and whisking to emulsify. Taste for salt and pepper, then pour the sauce over the haddock to serve.

Salmon Gravlax

This would have been a Viking recipe, not Anglo-Saxon, and has been traced back to 1348 according to the *Oxford Companion to Food*, but it is too good not to include here.

- **A side of salmon, about 450g–1.3kg (1–3lb)**
- **170g (6oz) honey or white or brown sugar**
- **Salt, to taste**
- **30g (1oz) chopped dill**
- **Mustard sauce, to serve**

Freeze the salmon for at least 3 days. Then thaw in the fridge.

Combine the honey or sugar, salt and chopped dill. In a baking dish, spread half of the salt-sugar mixture in one layer, then place the salmon on top, scattering with the rest of the salt-sugar mix. Cover the dish with cling film so that it touches the salmon completely (if it's easier, put the cling film in the dish before starting so you can wrap the salmon completely). Put tins or something heavy on top and place in the fridge. The longer it sits the harder and saltier it gets – 30 hours is good, but you can leave it for anywhere between 24 hours and 3 days. After this time the liquid will be expunged, which is the purpose of the weights.

Unwrap and rinse the salmon with water to get the salt off. Sprinkle with fresh dill and serve with a bought mustard sauce.

Side of Salmon: Slow-roasted, Seared and Hash

Cooking a side of salmon on a fire is much easier than cooking anything that walks. An animal with legs involves exponentially more time and a larger fire, for example, a lamb will need 6 hours and 10–12 logs easily. A side of salmon slow-roasted will be finished in 30–45 minutes (if you choose not to eat it raw). To slow-roast a piece of salmon as we imagine a Saxon might, place the salmon on a lever, like a shield, then lean the lever over the fire so it is not in direct flames but near low heat.

When you make a fire you want to have different heat zones – just like an oven you can turn up or down. Uhtred's people might not have made fires and then waited 2 hours until the embers were perfectly glowing; they might have made the fire and put the meat on the flames, so first flame to eating time would be short. Of course, a fire provides other services, like keeping one warm. A stew could be suspended over the fire and the shield with side of salmon leaning against the edges of fire.

Alternatively, a Saxon might have enjoyed the salmon over flames and cooked it like a marshmallow – that is, eaten it raw on the inside, but burned on the outside! Like all generations they probably liked the recipe they grew up with. A really nice piece of salmon is fatty, so it will be unctuous on the inside and crispy leathery on the outside.

Cooking a perfect piece of fish goes two ways. If the ingredient is so good why would you want to hide it? However, you may want to combine flavours and make a salmon hash or mash

148

with other flavours. Take a chunk of salmon, add chopped-up vegetables and make a succotash. Mix with your hands, then cook until the fish is a little browned.

This is camp cooking in your kitchen, but for a more modern version, you can cook the salmon slowly in a low oven or under a grill.

Lard-poached Salmon

Serves 6

- ❖ **1.3kg (3lb) skin-on salmon fillet**
- ❖ **120ml (4fl oz) lard or olive oil**
- ❖ **Salt and freshly ground black pepper**

Preheat the oven to 150°C/300°F/gas 2.

Place the salmon in a baking dish and rub lard or olive oil all over it. Sprinkle with salt and pepper. Roast until the edges are opaque and the fish is just cooked through, about 30 minutes.

Serve with leeks (see recipes for barley, leeks and peas on page 199 or cream-braised leeks with nutmeg on page 125) and a parsley salad.

Quick and Easy

- ❖ **120ml (4fl oz) olive oil**
- ❖ **675g (1½lb) skin-on salmon fillet**
- ❖ **A few dill sprigs**
- ❖ **Salt and freshly ground black pepper**

Preheat the oven to 245°C/475°F/gas 9.

Heat an ovenproof pan over high heat, then when hot, pour enough olive oil to cover the bottom of the pan and heat for 30 seconds. If the salmon is too large to fit into the pan, cut it in half, then place the fish, skin side up, in the hot oil for 2 minutes. Using a spatula, turn the salmon over and continue cooking for another 2–3 minutes, depending on thickness. Cover the top of the salmon with sprigs of dill, then place the pan in the oven for about 7 minutes until cooked through.

Salmon Hash

Serves 6
- ❖ **1.3kg (3lb) skin-on salmon fillet**
- ❖ **5–6 each of parsnips, turnips and carrots, peeled and chopped**
- ❖ **60ml (2½fl oz) olive oil**
- ❖ **Handful of fresh herbs, such as dill, savory, parsley or mint**
- ❖ **Salt and freshly ground black pepper**

Place the salmon and vegetables in a large pan, adding enough water to come halfway up the side of the salmon. Bring to a simmer, then cover and cook for 5–10 minutes depending on the thickness of the salmon. Do not overcook.

When the salmon is cooked, move it to a cutting board. Toss the lightly poached vegetables in a bit of olive oil before running them under a hot grill for a minute. The oil helps them char.

Flake the salmon, then toss with the vegetables and serve.

Turbot Poached in Butter

An early reference to the turbot can be found in a satirical poem 'The Emperor's Fish' by Juvenal, a Roman poet of the late first and early second centuries AD, suggesting this fish was a delicacy in the Roman Empire. The turbot is a large, left-eyed flatfish found primarily close to shore in sandy shallow waters throughout the Mediterranean, the Baltic Sea, the Black Sea and the North Atlantic. The European turbot has an asymmetrical disc-shaped body and has been known to grow up to 100cm (39in) long and 25kg (55lb) in weight.

The noblest fish in the sea are the turbot and the Dover sole. It takes 3–4 years for a turbot to grow to 30cm (12in). Its scarcity, combined with the particular finesse of its flesh, has meant that the turbot has been a highly sought-after and highly valued fish since ancient times – often regarded as the best of the flatfish.

- ❖ **225g (8oz) unsalted butter**
- ❖ **2–3 tablespoons water**
- ❖ **675g (1½lb) turbot**
- ❖ **Cider vinegar, to taste**

Melt the butter in a frying pan over low heat. Add the water and whisk until emulsified. Bring the liquid to a simmer and poach the turbot, meat side down. Turn, pull off the skin and continue poaching over gentle heat until the meat is done.

Whisk a little vinegar (to taste) into the butter sauce and spoon it over the fillet.

Braised Fillet of Turbot

- ❖ **250ml (8fl oz) white wine**
- ❖ **250ml (8fl oz) water**
- ❖ **Handful of fresh herbs, such as dill or thyme**
- ❖ **675g (1½lb) turbot fillets**
- ❖ **2 tablespoons butter**
- ❖ **1 tablespoon green sauce (see page 133)**

Put the wine and water together with the herbs in a pan and simmer for 5 minutes to infuse the liquid with the herbs.

Rest the pieces of turbot on top of the herbs, skin side up, then cover the pan and simmer for about 6 minutes, until the fish is cooked through.

Lift the fish onto a plate and keep warm. Add the butter to the pan and boil rapidly for 10 minutes to reduce the liquid and make a sauce.

To serve, peel the skin off the turbot and place the fish on a warmed plate. Stir the green sauce into the sauce to combine, and spoon over the fish.

THE GIFT OF GOD

In this story Uhtred is travelling across the lands
we now know as England, riding into the bitterly cold
winds of the North Sea towards Pritteuuella (Prittlewell,
Essex). He is with Alfred – probably the most important
man in Uhtred's life. The relationship between a pious
Christian king and a stubborn pagan warrior was never
going to be tranquil, but beneath the unlikely
friendship was intense mutual respect . . .

As I get older I am often asked about King Alfred.

He is famous, of course. Even the Danes who live in Northumbria are curious about his life, while the Christians are desperate to learn more.

So desperate that recently they sent a delegation from Contwaraburg to ask me about my memories of Alfred. They were led by a monk, a tall, skinny man called Brother Fricca who begged me for time so he could write down whatever I told him. I was annoyed by Brother Fricca's earnest questions and was in no mood to satisfy him. 'Alfred?' I said in a puzzled voice. 'Alfred? I remember a cobbler in Æbbanduna named Alfred. He made good boots.'

'King Alfred, lord!'

'Ah!' I pretended to think. 'Small fellow, lank hair, too thin.'

'Maybe a small fellow,' Brother Fricca said disapprovingly, 'but a great man all the same! Surely you agree?'

'Is that your opinion?'

'It is common knowledge, lord.'

'Then why ask me?'

'The archbishop,' Brother Fricca pressed on, 'will appeal to the Pope to have Alfred named as a saint!'

'King Alfred?' I pretended to be astonished. 'A saint?'

'Of course!'

'You can tell the Pope,' I said, 'that as a young man Alfred went through the kitchen maids like a hot seax through butter! He even had a bastard son by one of them, a good lad called Osbert.'

Brother Fricca had two other monks with him, both younger men who reddened at my words. One appeared to be about to make a note – he had brought a clean sheet of ass's skin, a pot of ink and some quills – but Brother Fricca slapped the quill aside.

'If that is true,' he said in a voice suggesting it was a lie, 'then that was before he discovered the saving grace of our redeemer.'

Brother Fricca must have noticed the hammer hanging at my neck and was probably already regretting his journey.

'If abandoning kitchen maids is a result of becoming a Christian,' I growled, 'then I'm glad I never did.'

Brother Fricca made the sign of the cross. 'It is well known,' he told me, 'that King Alfred enjoyed a happy marriage with the Lady Ealhswith,' he paused, 'and she is reckoned worthy of sainthood too, lord!'

'Ealhswith!' I was astonished. 'A saint? She was a bitch incarnate, a nagging, stupid woman who made poor Alfred's life a living misery. And you can write that down.'

He did not. Instead he looked at me with a severe expression. 'Lord,' he spoke patiently, 'the king and the archbishop have sent me to gather the true facts of the blessed King Alfred's life. The king expressly said you are one of the few men who stood beside him in battle and can vouch for his heroism. He told me you were a friend of King Alfred.'

'Alfred disliked me,' I said, 'and I disliked him. Does that sound like friendship to you?'

'The king insisted you were a friend to his grandfather,' Brother Fricca persisted.

The king, of course, was Æthelstan, who, since coming to the throne had become almost as pious as his grandfather. There had been a time when Æthelstan and I were close, indeed I had treated him almost as a son, but since he had claimed the throne of all Englaland he had ignored me. Now he had sent a skinny monk to scrape up my memories of long ago.

'We were companions,' I allowed.

'In battle, yes?'

'In war.'

'There's a difference?'

'If the god-damned Scots invade my land,' I said, 'there's war. If I take my warriors to slaughter the lot of them, that's battle.'

'God be thanked we are at peace with the Scots,' Brother Fricca said.

'We'll never be at peace with the bastards,' I said. 'Even as you're sitting here, wasting my time, there are probably a score of the hairy bastards plotting to attack this fortress with their men.'

Fricca's two companions peered anxiously around the great hall, half expecting to see brutal Scotsmen creeping in the shadows. Brother Fricca was made of sterner stuff and looked me in the eye.

'Lord,' he said plaintively, 'for King Alfred to be declared a saint, the Holy Father insists we provide proof of a miracle. You might be able to provide that proof?'

'Oh, I can,' I said, and all three monks brightened. 'The battle of Ethandun was a miracle! Just think of it! The Danes had captured all Britain except the marshes of Æthelingæg,

157

and Alfred scraped together a small army and beat the bastards at Ethandun. That was a miracle!'

'It was a sign of God's favour,' Brother Fricca said, 'but winning a battle is not considered a miracle. We have heard of the king restoring life to a young woman in Pritteuuella.' He paused to see if I recognised the name. I did, but said nothing. He sighed and pressed on. 'The gospels tell of our Lord raising the daughter of Jairus to life, and men in Wessex insist the king performed a similar miracle at Pritteuuella, and moreover many say you were with him.'

'I was.'

'Then be so good as to tell us what occurred.' Brother Fricca, armed with another clean skin, drew it towards him and dipped a quill in ink. It seemed there were to be three written accounts of the strange events that happened at Pritteuuella all those years ago.

Pritteuuella was a settlement east of Lundene and north of the Temes where the river widened to meet the sea. A few folk scratched a living there, growing wheat and barley, and keeping meagre herds of goats and sheep that grazed on the marshy fields. Despite its proximity to Lundene it was in East Anglia, which back then was ruled by Danish invaders, though the fisherfolk and farmers of Pritteuuella possessed nothing to attract raiders.

That all changed after King Alfred declared Lundene to be West Saxon, a decision that upset the Mercians, who had always claimed Lundene for their own, and the East Anglians who believed the old city to be in their territory. I had been sent to Lundene to command a small garrison to protect Alfred's newest territory, mostly by manning the city's walls, which had been conveniently left by the Romans. For a time life was uneventful until Alfred, typically, decided that the nailed god

required him to send missionaries into the East Anglian countryside to convert the Danish jarls who held the land. One of
those missionary outposts was established at Pritteuuella, and
I had obediently taken forty warriors to protect the monks,
who had built a small wooden church and a monastery beside
a stream which gave the settlement its name. We stayed there
for most of a summer and only left when the abbot declared
he no longer needed protection because the local Danish jarl
had declared himself to be Christian and was willing to give
the monks and nuns his pledge to keep them safe. The abbot,
revelling in his success in having turned a pagan warlord into
a dutiful Christian, wrote an exultant letter to Alfred saying
that the monastery of Pritteuuella was now in Christian land
and no longer in need of West Saxon warriors to defend its
territory. The warlord, Jarl Hoskuld, had declared himself
willing to be baptised.

Alfred, of course, was delighted and sent the abbot a generous gift of a large golden crucifix and accompanying altar
vessels made of silver. As if that weren't enough, he declared
that he would visit Pritteuuella to witness this success for
himself. And so he came to Lundene with fifty warriors and
almost as many priests and he dined at my home beside the
river in the east of the city. That night, out of courtesy, I wore
a cross instead of my usual hammer, and served a delicious
meal which, of course, Alfred could not eat. He suffered from
a stomach ailment and, on the advice of his doctors, ate dis-
gusting messes of boiled vegetables soaked in milk. Despite
his paltry meal it was a happy evening. Alfred was relaxed,
perhaps because I sat him next to Gisela, my wife, and she was
lively and funny, telling tales of her Danish childhood, which
Alfred enjoyed. I watched her over the table and thought how
beautiful she looked with her dark hair framing her long face

and bright eyes. She was plainly enjoying Alfred's company and he responded to her with obvious pleasure.

It was only after the meal that he turned to me with a grave face. 'You realise,' he said, 'that we will witness history?'

'History, lord?' I sawed a chunk of beef and tossed it to one of my dogs.

'We will witness the baptism of Jarl Hoskuld! By the grace of God,' Alfred exulted, 'an enemy has become a friend!'

'He's not the first,' I said, watching Alfred dilute a glass of wine with water. 'And usually,' I continued, 'they only convert to lull us into peace, and as soon as they have enough fighting men they go straight back to paganism.'

'That has happened,' Alfred conceded reluctantly, 'but Abbot Witulf assures me that Hoskuld's conversion is genuine. Hoskuld, he tells me, is filled with a new spirit of God. He and all his men are to be baptised!'

I let that pass. Alfred's companions, most of them priests, were echoing his delight and casting malevolent glances my way because none of them was convinced by the cross I wore. I ignored them and, next morning, led twenty of my men to join Alfred's fifty who were led by Steapa, an old friend.

'He's mad,' I told Steapa.

'Why?'

'Pritteuuella is enemy country,' I said, 'and Hoskuld, last time I heard, had over two hundred warriors.'

'Who have all agreed to be baptised,' Steapa said.

'And you believe that?'

'The king says it is true, so it must be.' There were times when I was tempted to think Steapa was stupid. He was a huge man who, when we first met, had been ordered to kill me, but since that failure he and I had become friends. He was not stupid, but there was a simplicity to him that could be irritating. Alfred trusted him, and Steapa was fearsome in his resolve to protect the king.

'Can you even imagine two hundred Danes lining up to be dunked in a river?' I asked.

'If their lord tells them to do that? Then yes.'

'Keep your mail on,' I advised him, 'and make sure that butcher's blade of yours is sharp.'

He touched the hilt of his massive sword. 'It's always sharp.'

I spurred ahead of him, cantering to join the dozen men I had ordered to ride a mile ahead of our party. They were scouts and they were spread across the countryside to search every copse, every field and every small settlement.

'Nothing to worry us,' Eadric assured me. He was the best of my scouts, a thin countryman with eyes better even than Finan's. 'They won't ambush us here,' he went on, 'land's too flat, lord. That's what worries me.' He nodded ahead where a high, tree-covered ridge reared up from the dull fields. 'The road climbs that slope,' Eadric went on, 'and if I was planning nonsense that's where I'd be.'

I looked southwards to where the Temes slid wide and grey between its low banks. I had suggested we travel to Pritteuuella by the river, but Alfred was prone to seasickness, even on calm water, and he was proud of his horsemanship, and so we were following the road east. But at the southern end of the ridge, where it fell towards the Temes, I could see a wide stretch of land no higher than where we rode, and I pointed to it. 'We go around the ridge, that way.'

'Good idea, lord,' Eadric said happily, 'we might live to see the sunset.'

Alfred galloped to join me. 'Why are we leaving the road?' he demanded.

'I don't like that ridge, lord,' I answered.

'We're safe!' he insisted. 'This is all Hoskuld's territory, is it not?'

'It is.'

'Then we are safe! The man has promised me his allegiance!'

'Then,' I said sourly, 'you should have demanded that he come to Lundene to be baptised.' In Lundene Hoskuld's followers would be outnumbered at least tenfold.

'We're forging a friendship,' Alfred said, 'and must demonstrate that we trust him.'

'Then we should have brought more men,' I growled. 'Besides, the horses are tired and by the time we reach that ridge top they'll be staggering.' That was not true, but it offered Alfred an excuse to accept my change in route. 'This way will be easier on the horses,' I went on, 'and won't add much time to the journey. We're close now, lord.'

He reluctantly accepted my decision, even though the detour around the southern end of the ridge was far from easy on the horses because the land was wet and crossed by ditches and blackthorn hedges. Alfred stopped to talk to two men laboriously clearing a ditch and asked them where we were. 'Pichesheye, lord,' one answered.

'Pichesheye,' Alfred repeated the name thoughtfully, then gave the two men an eager look. 'And you're Christians?'

'I think so, lord,' the man answered nervously.

'You have a priest?'

'He died, lord.'

'We shall send you another,' Alfred promised, 'the sheep must have a shepherd.' He spurred on.

I lingered. 'You know who that was?' I asked the two men. 'No, lord.'

'King Alfred of Wessex.' They glanced cautiously at the approaching warriors, but said nothing. Indeed, they looked puzzled and I reckoned they had never heard of Alfred. 'The king!' I said louder.

'Hoskuld, lord?' one said.

'Hoskuld is a jarl,' I said, 'and that man,' I pointed to Alfred, 'is the King of Wessex.'

I might as well have told them Alfred was the man in the moon. They had probably never heard of Wessex, and even if they had it was so impossibly remote from their muddy life on the northern bank of the Temes that it might as well have been on the moon. But at least, I thought sourly as I spurred after Alfred, Pichesheye was getting a new priest out of the encounter.

It was not late in the year, but that day was bitterly cold from an east wind scouring off the North Sea. 'Good thing we didn't come by ship,' Alfred greeted me when I caught up with him, 'it always seems colder on the water, don't you think?'

'It might seem colder, lord,' I said, 'but it's quicker. Besides, that cloak looks warm.'

'Ah, it is!' He was wearing a cloak made of broad red and white stripes that hung over his horse's rump and down to his boots. I could see the cloak was lined with fur, probably squirrel or possibly wolf. 'You need a cloak, Lord Uhtred,' he said.

'I have one, lord,' I gestured at my cloak that was tied to the back of my saddle, 'but it gets in the way of drawing a sword.'

He laughed at that. 'Always looking for a fight!'

I said nothing more and we rode for a mile or so in silence. I could see he was thoughtful and I guessed it was religion that was occupying his mind. My mind was on the ridge, looking for any sign that there were men on that high ground who might come swarming down the long slope to intercept us. I saw nothing, though the trees were so thick on the skyline that they could have hidden an army.

'I like your Gisela,' Alfred suddenly broke his silence.

'She's a good woman, lord,' I said.

He nodded. 'She has an,' he paused, looking for a word, 'an incisive mind.'

'She does, lord,' I said, and thought that Alfred's wife had an incisive tongue.

'She's a support to you?'

'Very much so, lord.'

He muttered something that sounded very like 'You're a lucky man', then spurred ahead again. I was so taken aback by the last scrap of conversation that I let him go, suspecting he wanted to be alone.

Finan caught up with me. 'He was trying to make a Christian out of you?' he asked, amused.

'He's given up on that.'

Steapa thundered past us on his huge stallion, evidently worried that his king was a solitary figure behind my scouts.

'He's not a happy man,' Finan said.

'Alfred?'

'Steapa.'

'Steapa?' I asked. 'He told me he believed Hoskuld is genuine. He thinks that when we get to Pritteuuella it's all going to be sweetness and Christian light.'

'And I think you put some doubt into his thick skull,' Finan remarked, and sure enough Steapa had evidently persuaded Alfred to ride with the main group of warriors.

Alfred confirmed it by calling to me as the two rode past us, 'I am to stay with my warriors, Lord Uhtred!'

'Every sheep needs a shepherd,' I said, and he laughed.

We rode on into the face of the bitter wind. To our right stretched the dull, soggy mass of the island of Caninga, then the land rose gently onto good pasture. This was Beamfleot, a place I would come to know only too well, but on that day there was nothing disturbing in the well-hedged farmland, or nothing disturbing until a pillar of smoke showed far ahead of us.

'A rick fire?' Finan guessed.

'Let's hope it's nothing more than that.'

The smoke served as a beacon for us and, as we drew closer, it faded as the fire that fed it died away.

Alfred caught up with me again. 'I pray that's not Pritteuuella,' he said anxiously.

'Maybe just a rick fire, lord,' I answered.

'Maybe,' he sounded dubious. 'You've met Hoskuld?' he asked.

He had asked that question twice the previous evening and I gave him the same answer. 'I've fought his men, but never met him.'

'He was a troublesome warrior,' the king observed, and I noted he had said 'was', meaning that he still believed Hoskuld's conversion was genuine, thus changing a Danish enemy into a Christian ally.

'He's a troublemaker,' I said curtly. 'He brought two ships to the Blakewat a dozen years ago, slaughtered every landowner within twenty miles, attracted more followers, and now rules most of southern East Anglia.'

'A capable man, then.' Alfred sounded nervous.

'He wants Lundene,' I said, 'which is why I know of him. He's sent raiding parties to the city's boundaries and we've driven them off.'

'He hasn't the strength to capture Lundene,' Alfred said, still nervously.

'Not now,' I said, 'but as he gets richer he attracts more men.'

'That danger is past,' Alfred reassured himself. 'Within days, Lord Uhtred, we shall count all of Hoskuld's land as part of Christian Englaland.'

I almost laughed at that. Alfred had started to use the name Englaland to describe all the regions where folk spoke our language, which, to Alfred, meant that they belonged to the same tribe. His dream was to unite all those folk into one country, Englaland. I thought it was a nonsense. It was possible that the Ænglish speakers of East Anglia might welcome deliverance from their Danish conquerors, but I could not see the Mercians or my own Northumbrians abandoning old loyalties to accept a king from Wessex.

'To make Englaland,' I pointed out, 'you'll need to fight all the way to the Scottish border, and I can't see the Scots being happy about that.'

'The Scots are good Christians,' Alfred said, 'and will welcome us. Better to have Christians on their border than pagans.'

I almost laughed aloud again. I suppose it is good for kings to have ambitious dreams, but that Alfred truly thought the Scots would be pleased to have a mighty Saxon kingdom to their south just because it was Christian, defied belief. The Scots were like wolves, savage and forever hungry, and they did not care what god was worshipped by the owners of the cattle they stole.

'One small thing concerns me,' Alfred continued.

'Which is, lord?'

'It seems that Hoskuld's reason for becoming a Christian is a belief that the true God is stronger than his pagan gods and will give him victory in battle. Which is true, of course, but God is also the prince of peace. I must talk to him about that.'

Hoskuld probably believed that the nailed god was more

powerful than his gods because his forces had been routinely whipped by my men. But at least half of my men, like me, were pagans, which confused the argument. It seemed tactful not to discuss that with Alfred who, as we neared Pritteuuella, became both elated and troubled.

Elated because the baptism of Hoskuld marked a triumph in his campaign to convert the Danes from pagan enemies into Christian allies, and troubled because I had scorned that hope. My scorn was abetted by the smoke that still drifted towards us on the cold wind. Alfred clung to the belief that it was a rick fire or, at worst, a blaze at one of the many farm-steads around Pritteuuella. Cenwulf, one of my men, knew the area and assured the king that there were at least a dozen substantial settlements nearby, but as we drew closer Alfred's anxiety grew stronger.

'When I was a child,' I told Alfred, 'we used to make caves in hayricks.'

'Why?' he asked sharply.

'Mainly as a place to hide with girls,' I said, astonished that he had even asked, 'and sometimes we lit fires in them.'

'That was unforgivably stupid,' he retorted.

'It was,' I agreed, 'I still remember the thrashing my father gave me.'

He grunted at that. We were skirting a creek that twisted from the wide river and his horse stumbled, almost unsad-dling the king. He recovered himself and patted the stallion's neck. 'It must be an accidental fire,' he said, and spurred on.

I let him go. A half-dozen of his own men rode with Alfred, but Steapa, their commander, fell in beside me.

'He's not happy.'

'He's only happy when he's praying,' I said sourly.

'He was looking forward to this journey.'

167

'So he can pray over Hoskuld?'

'He was looking forward to seeing you,' Steapa said, 'for some reason he likes you.'

I said nothing.

'Of course he wants to convert you too,' Steapa went on.

'I'm a baptised Christian,' I said defensively, and I suppose that was true. Indeed I had been baptised twice, the second time at my brother's death when I had inherited the name Uhtred. The church declared that no one could be baptised more than once, so I deduced I had been washed into the religion the first time and washed out the second.

Steapa ignored my claim. 'The Lady Ealhswith had a dream,' he said instead.

'Of food?' I asked nastily. Alfred's wife was an enthusiastic eater. While her husband spooned his horrible vegetable messes she consumed the finest meats.

'That this journey would end badly,' Steapa said, 'and it worried the king.'

'Anything that woman said would worry me,' I remarked. I did not like Ealhswith and she did not like me. She was a bitter woman, perhaps most bitter that the West Saxons did not honour the king's wife with the title of queen. That was perverse, I thought, but I was happy enough that the sour Ealhswith was denied the title. 'If the king is unhappy about anything,' I said forcibly, 'it's Ealhswith.'

Steapa said nothing at first. I suspect he agreed with me, but was too loyal to Alfred to criticise Ealhswith, but then he nodded. 'The woman has been giving him a bad time,' he said it softly, so I almost didn't hear him over the sigh of the wind in the grass. 'He wanted her to come as far as Lundene,' Steapa went on, a bit louder, 'but she said she wouldn't meet you. Says you're a bad influence on the king.'

'I do try to be,' I said mischievously.

'He doesn't understand warriors,' Steapa said, nodding at the king who was now a half-mile ahead of us. 'He knows he needs us, but wishes he didn't.'

'We should catch up with him,' I said, and we put spurs to our horses and galloped up a slight slope beyond which Alfred had vanished among low trees.

The trees must have been planted as a windbreak to protect a small steading, which we galloped past to find Alfred on the far side of the trees. Most of my scouts were there, and Cenwulf was among them. He rode to my side and nodded towards the burning buildings a mile or so ahead. 'That's Pritteuuella, lord,' he said in a low voice.

The monastery had once contained a church, a barn, and other buildings where the monks slept and ate. From our vantage point on the low ridge it seemed as if all those wooden buildings had been set ablaze, all but one, a small house that lay a bowshot to the south of the burning buildings. That one house was quite different, to my eyes it looked Roman with its white walls and tiled roof. It showed no sign of burning, no smoke came from the shuttered windows or through the roof and, while my men waited with the king on the low ridge, Finan and I spurred to that one remaining building, the small Roman house. I told Alfred we were scouting and that he should wait till we were sure no enemies were in the area.

I had always been fascinated by the buildings the Romans left behind. They were so well made, so impressive and, at the same time, deeply saddening because it was obvious, at least to me, that we could build nothing to compare. The Romans left us soaring temples, massive ramparts and airy, comfortable houses like the one I occupied in Lundene. The roofs actually kept out the rain! The small building at Pritteuuella was the same and I guessed it had been a farmstead. It had a paved yard at the front where a porch faced towards a small stream, and behind it were three or four rooms. As I dismounted and walked onto the porch I saw that the walls had been covered in white plaster that now was cracked and broken, revealing bricks beneath. That made sense to me; the land in this corner of East Anglia had no stone for building, but was rich in clay that could be baked into bricks. Finan had followed me and stepped through the open door first. 'The monks used the place,' he said, pointing to a wooden crucifix that had evidently been pulled from a wall of the great room.

'They'd be stupid not to,' I said.

'Probably the abbot lived here,' Finan suggested, 'the top dog usually gets the best kennel.'

The enemy had been here, for the furniture had been broken, and against one wall was a massive wooden chest that had been ransacked. All that was left of its contents were some threadbare cloaks and a richly embroidered scapula, which surprised me because the Danes liked such trifles.

'They didn't try to burn the place,' I said idly.

'The bastard will want to keep it,' Finan said. 'If he rules this territory, he'll want a home down here.'

The room with the emptied chest had evidently been the abbot's dining room for it contained a table, six chairs and a hearth that had been crudely hacked through one of the outside walls. A fire there, I reflected, would as likely fill the room with smoke as heat it, but wherever we used Roman buildings we made such crude changes.

'No one here.' Finan had gone into the next room, a small kitchen with another makeshift hearth. Plates, jugs and bowls had all been smashed to litter the floor with shards.

'We should get back to the king,' I said.

'You go,' Finan said, 'I want to scratch around here.'

'You think they'll have left you anything?' I asked, amused.

'Luck of the Irish,' he said.

'I'll want half.'

'How lucky are you?'

'Don't stay long,' I admonished him and went back to my horse.

I rode back, swerving close to the burning monastery where the flames were low as they consumed the last timbers. There was no one in sight, nobody trying to extinguish the fires or even just standing to gawp at the destruction. No enemy either, if indeed it had been an enemy who set the fires, and it seemed most unlikely to me that it could have been an accident. An accident might burn one building, but all of them?

I rode to where Alfred and his men watched from the ridge. 'You stay here, lord King,' I called to him.

'Lord Uhtred . . .' he began.

'They might have left men there,' I said, though I knew that was not true. I also knew that what he would see would probably drive him into a rage. 'Cenwulf! Bring all the scouts!' I turned to Alfred, 'I'll send for you, lord.'

He just nodded. He looked so bleak as he gazed at the destruction of his dream, and I felt a stab of pity for him.

'Let's go,' I said to Steapa, and we spurred our horses, drew our swords, and raced towards the embers of Alfred's hope.

Brother Fricca had listened to the story so far without comment, just scratching notes with his quill, but now he held up a thin, ink-stained hand. 'There is something here I do not understand,' he said in a puzzled voice.

'What?' I asked.

'You assumed that the fire was caused deliberately, by an enemy. Why?'

'Because all the buildings were ablaze, that's why.'

'I still do not understand,' he went on.

'How many farmsteads have you burned?' I asked.

'None, of course,' he replied primly.

'I've burned dozens,' I said, 'and you don't just set one building ablaze, you torch them all.'

'But fires spread, do they not?'

'They do,' I allowed, 'and there was plenty of wind that day, but there were supposedly forty or fifty monks at Pritteuuella, and if one building had caught fire then they'd have clawed the thatch from the others with hooks and rakes. And they could have soaked the walls with water, and the one thing Pritteuuella didn't lack was water. I assume the poor bastards had buckets.'

Brother Fricca blanched at the word 'bastards', but bowed his head. 'I acknowledge your superior experience of destruction, Lord Uhtred, but am disturbed by your suggestions that King Alfred was less than happily married.'

'Dear God,' I said, 'did you ever meet the Lady Ealhswith?'

'I never had that privilege.'

'Be glad of that,' I said, 'the bitch had a tongue that could slice leather.'

'We have witnesses that speak of the deep and holy affection that reigned between them,' Brother Fricca challenged me.

'Well they spawned enough children,' I allowed, 'so she wasn't entirely useless.'

'You did not like her,' he said, as if that was the cause of my ugly words.

'I detested her,' I said, 'and she detested me.'

'With reason,' he said.

'Reason?'

'You were a pagan!' He spat the last word as if it was sour on his tongue.

'And still am,' I said, 'but I note that none of you have rejected my hospitality, my food or my ale.'

'We are doing God's work,' Brother Fricca observed.

'Ealhswith used to say that,' I said, 'and most of God's work for her was nagging her husband. Now, do you want me to tell you the tale or argue about a woman I regrettably knew well and who you never met?'

Brother Fricca dipped his quill in ink and nodded to me. 'Pray continue, Lord Uhtred.'

Lord Uhtred continued.

They were all dead. The monks, in their dull brown robes, lay about the burning buildings in blood-soaked horror. All of them. We searched to discover one who might yet live, but whoever had attacked the monastery had made certain there were no survivors. The second largest building which had probably been the main living quarters was still burning fiercely, though the southern end of it, nearest the distant Temes, was still standing. There was the smell of burned flesh, which suggested that many of the monks had been trapped inside or had been tossed into the fires by the enemy, and I had no doubt who that enemy was.

'Hoskuld,' I said to Steapa.

'Or one of his enemies,' Steapa said, trying to preserve a vestige of Alfred's hopes.

'Hoskuld,' I said again, and I sent Cenwulf back to summon

Alfred, 'but warn the king he's not going to like what he sees here.'

Alfred rode through the drifting smoke and, for a moment, I thought he was about to vomit. His anger was evident, a fury that made him speechless for minutes and kept men away from him as he walked his horse among the slain monks. 'Who did this?' were his first words addressed to me.

'I assume Hoskuld,' I said.

'You don't know that,' he said harshly.

'What we know, lord,' I said, 'is that the killers came from the north. There were a lot of them, and before they attacked they sent a smaller group looping around to the south to cut off the escape of the monks. The nearest Danes to the north are Hoskuld's men.'

'How can you know that?'

I gestured at Cenwulf. 'He followed the tracks of their horses, lord. He's good at that.'

Alfred grunted, then looked at Steapa, and then at me again. 'If this is Hoskuld,' he said coldly, 'he must die.'

'He will, lord,' I said just as coldly.

The rest of our warriors had come to the burning monastery and Alfred pointed at the corpses. 'They must be buried,' he ordered, 'and the fires extinguished.' He dismounted and looked up at me. 'This might have been done by other Danes,' he said, 'men who disapprove of Hoskuld's conversion.'

'Possible,' I said dubiously, 'but Hoskuld should have been here ready to greet you, and we haven't found any Danish bodies. If one of his enemies mounted the attack they'd have killed Hoskuld and his men along with the monks.'

'If it was Hoskuld, then he deceived us,' Alfred conceded reluctantly, 'but why not wait for our arrival before killing?'

'We have enough warriors to hurt him badly,' I said, 'and

Danes are ever reluctant to lose men. I doubt he brought all his warriors, a hundred would be more than enough. You would have been a trophy for him, but he was more interested in the silver and gold.'

Alfred turned to look at the church where flames still showed. He said nothing.

'You sent Abbot Witulf valuable treasures,' I went on, 'and I'll wager you'll find no melted silver or gold in those ruins.'

'You will find the truth of this sacrilege, Lord Uhtred,' Alfred said sternly, 'and bring Hoskuld to me at Wintanceaster, where he will die.'

'Yes, lord,' I said and just then Finan called from the small Roman building, 'There's a live one here!'

'What did he say?' Alfred asked.

'He's found a survivor,' I said, and spurred towards the farmstead.

Finan had gone back indoors and I followed him. 'It's a lass,' he said, 'poor thing.'

He led me into a room that was dark because the shutters were closed.

'The abbot's bedroom,' Finan said, and I saw another wooden crucifix had been ripped from the plastered wall, and then heard a whining that appeared to come from a low bed.

'A dog?' I asked, disappointed.

'A girl,' Finan said, and I heard a low moan.

'Open the shutters,' I said, and in the new light saw that the whining had come from a dog, a small terrier bitch that was bleeding from a cut to her stomach. I reached in to pull the wretched animal out of a pool of blood, then went still. 'Poor girl,' I said.

The dog had bled all over a piece of white cloth which I now saw was the dress of a young woman. In the dark shadows she had been almost invisible, but as Finan pushed open the last shutter I saw the girl move her hand towards me as if reaching for help. I took her hand and held it and she moaned again and seemed to try to move towards me, so I put my left hand beneath her thin shoulders to cradle her. As I slid my hand beneath her thin body my fingers caught on a leather thong around her neck. I pulled on it and it snapped and a pendant fell into my hand. I stuffed it into a pouch at my belt, then drew her towards me. 'You're going to live,' I told her, though judging by the blood on her thin dress that was unlikely. The dress, a linen shift, was soaked in blood, and more blood smeared her face and had stiffened in her light golden hair.

Alfred had come into the room. He took one look at the girl then went to one of the open windows. 'Father Herebald!' he shouted, 'Father Herebald!' He glanced at me. 'Father Herebald is a healer.'

I looked down at the girl who might have been seventeen or eighteen years old. Her eyes were closed, she was shivering, and I heard her give a small moan. Her skin was pale, white as the wall's flaking plaster. The dog whined and struggled to be beside her, but the poor beast was plainly dying and I was grateful when Finan carried her away.

'She must live,' Alfred said. He knelt beside me and for a moment I thought he was talking of the dog and was about to dash his hopes when I realised he spoke of the girl. He was stroking her face, that part which was not covered in blood, and muttering soothing words. Her face was very pale, but as I looked at her I was struck by her beauty. It was a thin, strong face and when, momentarily, she opened her eyes they were bright blue. She only kept them open for a heartbeat and almost screamed in fear when she saw us, but Alfred's gentle words and soft caress seemed to reassure her. 'Let me take her,' Alfred urged me, and I gently took my arm from her shoulders and let the king take my place.

Father Herebald was a tall, skinny priest of some forty or more years who knelt beside the king. 'We must take her to shelter, lord, and warm her.'

'This is the only shelter,' Alfred snapped, annoyed.

'She needs warmth, lord.' Herebald had touched the girl's face that was cold.

'Then make a fire in here,' Alfred said curtly. The girl moaned again, perhaps scared by the asperity in Alfred's voice, and he stroked her cheek and murmured softly to her.

'We need water, lord,' Father Herebald said nervously.

'One of you fetch water,' Alfred ordered the men crowding into the room, 'and the rest of you go!'

They left reluctantly. I stayed and Alfred did not command me to leave. I stood above the bed where Alfred knelt, his hand in the girl's hand, and he told her she would live, that her wounds would be healed, 'And you will be happy again.' He said it over and over, stroking her cheek.

Father Herebald stood by nervously, peering down at the shivering girl, who suddenly moaned again, the moan interrupted by a choking sound, and her whole body stiffened and then relaxed.

'I fear, lord,' Father Herebald began, then hesitated

'Speak up, Father,' Alfred said.

'She may have just died, lord.'

'Nonsense!

'Permit me, lord,' the priest said and reached down to feel the girl's wrist and then he put a finger on her neck. The priest's face crumpled. 'Lord,' he said, and did not dare say more.

'Lord Uhtred!' Alfred backed away from the bed.

'Lord?'

'You have experience of death. Tell me if she lives.'

I was reluctant, but I knelt where the king had been and placed a thumb and finger either side of her neck. Her skin was warm, but I felt no pulse. 'Bring me fire and a feather,' I told Father Herebald and he seemed grateful for the order, which took him out of the room. He returned a few moments later with the feather of a seagull and a piece of wood that smouldered at one end. 'I will do it,' he said.

I made way for him. He lit the feather's tip and I caught a whiff of the foul smell, then he waved it beneath the girl's nostrils. She showed no response and the priest snatched the feather away before its burning scraps fell on her pale skin.

'I'm sorry, lord,' he spoke reluctantly, 'but she is dead.'

'No!' Alfred said. 'No!'

A second priest brought a pail of water and Alfred used a cloth to clean the girl's face of blood, then tried to wash the blood from her fair hair. 'I see no wound,' he said.

Father Herebald knelt and gently moved the girl's hair. 'She has been hit here, a woeful blow, lord.' He parted the bright gold hair to show Alfred a crusted line of blood on her scalp.

'The skull is not broken?' Alfred asked.

'It seems not, lord,' Herebald was pressing his fingers along the bloody line, 'but she was hit hard.'

'And where else is she wounded?' Alfred demanded, gesturing at the blood-soaked linen shift.

'We must,' Father Herebald began, then his voice faltered.

'Undress her?' the king snapped the question, obviously annoyed by the priest's hesitance. 'Of course we must. Lord Uhtred?'

'Lord?' I thought he was going to demand that I leave.

I was wrong. 'You have a knife?'

'Of course, lord.'

I pulled out the small knife I used for eating and took hold of the girl's shift at her neck, then slit it down to the hem at her feet.

'Wash her,' Alfred ordered Father Herebald, and the priest nervously used a water-soaked cloth to clean the blood from her pale body. He turned her over to inspect her back, then finished cleaning her belly and thighs.

There was no wound, none. The blood on the shift must have come from the dog, and once she was clean I was staring at a young girl of such astonishing beauty that I felt I was somehow trespassing. I did not want to be there, yet I could not take my eyes from her slender body that was so perfect, so deathly pale and untouched. Alfred must have felt something like I did because he took his hand from hers and made the sign of the cross.

'She is an angel!' he said. 'An angel!'

'A dead angel,' I muttered.

My words annoyed Alfred. 'She is not dead,' he said firmly, 'just sleeping.' He stood and took off his gaudy red and white cloak with its fur lining and laid it over her body. 'We will make a fire in here,' he said, 'and pray for her. I thank you, Lord Uhtred, and hope you add your prayers to ours.'

'Of course, lord,' I said, knowing I was dismissed and wondering whether Alfred really had demanded that I pray to my gods. If so it was an astonishing remark and I was still amazed by it when Finan joined me outside the half-burned building.

'What's happening?'

'Alfred won't believe she's dead.'

Finan shrugged. 'What was a girl doing at a monastery?'

'Who knows? Maybe she's the daughter of one of the workers here?'

'They're all dead too. Poor thing would be better off joining them.'

'Don't tell Alfred that. He's praying for her.'

'Christ!' Finan said. 'How long will that take?'

'All night?' I suggested.

'Then we'd better make sure we're safe,' Finan said, 'because whoever did this can't be far away.'

I nodded, and just then Father Herebald came from the abbot's chamber holding the torn bloody shift. He sighed. 'I have to wash it,' he said helplessly, 'and the king commands that you set guards around the monastery, lord.'

'All night?'

'So he said. And I'm to find food.' Father Herebald looked close to tears. 'He keeps saying the same thing over and over.'

'What?'

'*Non est mortua puella, sed dormit.*' I must have looked blank because the priest translated for me, 'The girl isn't dead, just sleeping! They're the words of our Lord in Luke's gospel. Then he tells her to get up, *Puella, surge!*'

'He's lost his mind,' Finan said quietly.

'If you could see her,' I told him, 'you'd understand. She's . . .' I hesitated, not knowing what word I wanted, 'beautiful,' I finished lamely. 'She's just beautiful.'

In truth I did not quote the Latin words from Luke's gospel to Brother Fricca. Instead I told him that Alfred had spoken in Latin and that the only word I remembered was *puella*. I remembered it only because Father Beocca had tried to teach me Latin, which was about as much use as trying to teach a horse to forge iron, and the word for a girl had stuck in my head. It greatly excited Brother Fricca who immediately quoted the correct words to me, or at least I thought they were correct, and he clasped his inky hands together and raised his eyes to the hall's rafters where the banners of my defeated enemies hung. 'They are the very words of our Saviour! He spoke them when he raised a child from the dead!'

One of the younger priests, a stern-looking youth with thick black hair, peered at me. 'Are you certain, Lord Uhtred, that the girl was dead?'

'I'm certain,' I said curtly.

'Maybe the girl slept deeply?' the young monk persisted.

'Silence!' Brother Fricca said angrily. 'Lord Uhtred was present and he has borne witness to us. Her skin was deathly pale, there was no pulse, and no evidence of breath! Does that sound like sleep to you?'

The young monk shrugged and for a moment looked as if he would argue, then he inclined his head and agreed with Fricca. 'It sounds like death, brother.'

'Indeed it does! You agree, lord?'

I nodded slowly. 'I agree.' I took a breath. 'I didn't want her to be dead, I truly wanted some flicker of life. She was so extraordinarily beautiful and so fragile. I've never forgotten her, never will. But,' I paused, remembering that pale naked body, so slender and perfect, her skin unmarked, her face oddly calm after the savagery of the day, 'but,' I went on, 'she was dead. I think she was alive when I first saw her, but died soon after.'

'And Father Herebald, you say he was a healer?'

'He was.'

'And he believed her to be dead?'

'He did.'

'Then we may accept that as evidence of the truth,' Brother Fricca said firmly. 'So you guarded the chamber where the girl lay?'

181

'No,' I said. 'Six of Steapa's men did that, the rest of us went after the raiders.'

It was late in the day when we left the smouldering embers of Pritteuuella to follow the tracks northwards. The decision to leave the monastery was mine as Alfred would not leave the abbot's house or the girl's corpse. I had shouted through the door to tell him what we were doing, but the only response was a grunt. So we left.

It was a chill evening as we rode north. The hoofprints were easy to follow, going straight to the southern bank of the River Roch where the enemy had crossed a ford. The tide was rising, swirling water between the muddy banks, but we forced our way through the river and rode on as the light failed until we came to the larger River Cruc.

There was another ford, but the water was now too high for safe crossing and the sun had set. We saw no men on the further bank, and I was satisfied that Hoskuld had left no forces between the Cruc and Pritteuuella and so turned for home. I knew that Hoskuld's steading was at Mældun, some miles north of the Cruc, and guessed he had retreated there. I doubted he would come back to attack us. He must have known we had a considerable force, not as large as he could muster, but enough to hurt him badly even if he defeated us. He would gain some precious armour and weapons with such a victory, but nothing to compare with the silver and gold his treachery had won him from the monastery, and he risked losing a significant number of his own troops in a battle with us.

'He had retreated to his fortress,' I told Fricca.

'And you did not confront him?'

'It was almost night-time, the ford was too deep, and I had less than half the number of men Hoskuld had, so no, I decided to live.'

'And Alfred stayed with the girl.'

'He did.

'Praying.'

'Praying,' I confirmed. And so he was.

Steapa's men had made a small hearth in the abbot's bed-chamber and punched a hole in the tiled roof so the smoke could escape. The smoke twisted out of the hole and the small flames lit the chamber's interior. Once back at the monastery I found Steapa sitting by the farmstead's door. The shutters of the bedroom's windows had been closed again. I told him to snatch some sleep. 'I'll guard the door.'

'He wants no one to enter,' Steapa said in a low voice.

'I'll make sure of that.'

'He's still awake,' Steapa said, then heaved himself to his feet and went to find food and sleep.

I sat with my back leaning on the wall beneath one of the shuttered windows and, as the night finally fell I could hear Alfred's voice speaking low. He was offering the girl endear-ments and sometimes talking to his god passionately. Finan had joined me, bringing a hunk of bread, cheese and a pot of ale.

'What's happening?' he asked as he settled beside me.

'Nothing,' I said.

'Who's there?' Alfred asked from inside the chamber.

'Lord Uhtred and Finan,' I answered.

He just grunted in response and then fell silent. After a while his voice sounded again, though so low I could not make out his words, but the tone was the same. He was com-forting the dead girl and praying to his god. I even fell asleep at some point, an offence for which I would have punished any of my men who did the same while on guard duty.

I was woken by Finan who poked me painfully in the leg. 'Listen!' he hissed to me.

I listened. I heard Alfred say, 'You will live, Godifu! Live a long life!'

'Godifu?' I whispered.

'Just listen,' Finan insisted, and I heard the girl give a low moan. I gazed at Finan in the wan moonlight and saw astonishment on his face.

'She lives?' I asked in a low whisper, but with an astonishment equal to Finan's.

'She lives!' Finan said. 'Listen!'

Godifu, if that was her name, spoke in a very low voice, too low to hear properly, but she was speaking. It was a weak voice, a voice of pain, but she was answering Alfred's urgent questions. I could make out his words, asking where she came from, what had brought her to the monastery, and what had happened to her. Who were her parents? Was she hungry? Did she trust God? She did not answer every question, but enough of them, and once or twice I heard her moan in pain.

Finan and I stayed very still, both listening, hearing the two voices that were almost drowned by the sound of the small stream and the sigh of wind over the marshes. I remember looking up at the stars and touching the hammer hanging at my neck, and I remember thinking that the girl could not have been dead, that I had been mistaken, but another part of me insisted I had been right and that Alfred's prayers had brought her to life. I was in awe and bemusement. I had argued with Father Beocca so often, saying that if the Christian god was truly the one god and all powerful then why did he not show us his power with miracles? Father Beocca, irritated by my stubborn scorn, had insisted that Christ's gospel miracles were sufficient, and if we were so blind to their wonder then we deserved nothing but hell. Now, it seemed, I was hearing proof of a new miracle. Godifu lived.

'She must have been sleeping,' I whispered to Finan.

'You really believe that?' he whispered back.

I shook my head. I still did not understand, but spoke the truth. 'I'm sure she was dead.'

'She's not now!'

'Lord Uhtred!' Alfred's voice called. 'Are you still there?'

'I am, lord King!'

'Some broth and ale. Maybe a little bread.'

'Yes, lord.'

I told Finan to stay and went to find the food. The men who were camped around the smouldering monastery had boiled some salt beef we had brought with us, and I managed to kindle a small fire and heat a pot with the remnants of that meal. I found bread and tore it into hunks that I dropped into the pot and, when the mixture was hot, I poured it into a jug. I could find no ale, but discovered a spoon, which I carried with the jug back to the house. I carried the jug into the big chamber and rapped on the bedroom door.

'Lord King? Your food!'

'Wait!' Alfred ordered.

I waited a short time, then the door was cautiously pushed open. Alfred faced me, barefoot and dressed only in a thin shirt. That surprised me because Alfred was a most fastidious man who dressed carefully. I had never seen him half-dressed and my astonishment almost made me drop the precious jug. 'I'm sorry, lord, I couldn't find ale.'

'It doesn't matter. Go, and thank you.' He was in a hurry and took the big jug from me with both hands. 'And close the door,' he added.

I had a brief chance to see into the room before I pushed the door shut. I saw the girl, covered with Alfred's cloak, staring at me, her eyes bright in the light of the fire. She was alive, I saw her blink, but I also had an impression of something else. The bed was against the far wall and she was occupying the far side of it and, where the piled cloaks had been peeled back I got a sense that someone had just climbed from that bed. I rammed the door shut then went outside and sat beneath the window again. Finan had seen through the door at the same time I did and now looked at me with a quizzical expression. I just shook my head.

'None of our business,' I muttered.

I looked back to the stars and thought what tricky bastards the gods were, then thought about the girl's name, Godifu, which meant 'gift from God'.

'Gift from God,' Brother Fricca said in a voice of awe, 'then this is the same story we've heard in Wintanceaster, and it's true!'

'True?' I asked.

'She died and was brought back to life! You are the witness!'

'You are certain she was dead?' the young monk with the thick black hair asked, to Brother Fricca's evident disapproval.

'I am sure she was dead,' I answered, 'and I believe I saw her die.'

The young priest frowned. 'Have you ever seen another dead person brought to life?'

'Not like that,' I answered, 'but after every battle we pile the dead for burning, and usually one or two cough or call out.'

'But that is the chaos of battle,' Brother Fricca said. 'This was different.'

'It was different,' I said, 'I saw her dead and then alive.'

'You're certain?' the young priest persisted.

'I'm certain,' I confirmed, and looked at the young priest, 'dead girls don't blink,' I told him.

'They don't speak either,' Brother Fricca said firmly, 'and you heard her speak.'

'I did, but I couldn't hear what she said,' I hesitated, 'the king told me later he had found her difficult to understand.'

'Not surprising,' Brother Fricca said dismissively, 'she had been wounded and the East Anglians speak in a barbarous fashion.'

'He told me,' I went on, 'that he could not really catch her name, but decided it was Godifu.' Which meant, I thought, that Alfred had given her the name himself.

'Of course it was Godifu,' Brother Fricca said, 'everyone knows that name!'

Which is true because Godifu, whom people now call Saint Godifu though the Pope in Rome has never accepted her sainthood, is buried in the great church Alfred built in Wintanceaster. Pilgrims visit her tomb and pray to her, and it is said that Alfred himself knelt at that tomb every day of his life.

'If our mission is successful,' Brother Fricca told me, 'then the holy father in Rome will accept Godifu's sainthood along with the king's. We must pray for that.'

'But Godifu died that night?' the young priest asked.

'She died again at dawn,' I said. I still remember Alfred's tears. He was sobbing and that sound made us enter the room where he was embracing the girl and crying into her hair. I very gently prised him away and held him in my arms while Finan felt the girl's face and neck.

'Cold,' he said. He made the sign of the cross. 'She's gone to heaven, lord King.'

'Where I will meet her again,' Alfred insisted, and I hope he did because sharing eternity with his wife would have turned heaven into hell.

Alfred had insisted that Godifu's body was wrapped tightly and carried to Wintanceaster where she was buried in a service conducted by the Archbishop of Contwaraburg. Alfred never claimed that he had performed a miracle, all he said when asked about Godifu was that she was an angel sent from heaven who had died because the pagans killed her, and that tale was enough, though the rumour of her two deaths and brief resurrection spread through all Wessex.

'What was the blessed Godifu doing at Pritteuuella?' the young monk asked me.

'She told Alfred that she had taken her small dog to the monastery where there was a famed healer,' I said.

'Did the dog live?'

I shook my head. 'It's buried with her.'

That was almost the final question the monks asked me before they hurried south to carry their good news to Contwaraburg and from there, I suppose, to Rome. I have heard nothing of their mission since, nor do I care. Alfred was a good man and good men are rare enough, so I suppose he deserves sainthood, though he was also capable of great cruelty.

In time we did capture Hoskuld by luring him to a monastery in Berecingas, which lay not far to the east of Lundene. We lured him with tales of the monastery's wealth and he fell into our trap. I took him to Wintanceaster where his presence put Alfred into a cold rage. He had Hoskuld stripped naked and whipped till he confessed that he had ransacked Pritteuuella, then Alfred decreed that he should die as the monks had died. He watched Hoskuld scream and writhe as he was slowly roasted to death. Alfred then took me to his great church and scattered some of the dead man's ashes on Godifu's marble tomb.

'It is over,' he said, 'and God's justice is done.' He paused and touched my arm. 'I sincerely believe,' he told me, 'that she was an angel sent from heaven.'

I remembered that slim white body, so beautiful in that place of smoke-stinking slaughter. 'I am sure you are right, lord King,' I said, and that was the last time he mentioned Godifu to me. He did not like to speak of what happened on that night in Pritteuuella, and so I did not tell him Godifu's last secret, which was that around her neck the perfect angel, the gift of God, had worn a small silver hammer.

I have it still.

Part Three

STORAGE

Historical Background

The question of how food was stored during this time is a fascinating one. To get through the winters was essential for every household, rich or poor, and without the convenience of refrigeration, one either had to survive only on fresh seasonal food or learn the skills of food preservation. So, how did the Anglo-Saxons keep food for any length of time?

Firstly, a suitable place to store food was one of the most important attributes of any Anglo-Saxon household. While a castle or hall would have cold underground cellars and walled rooms often with stone shelves, which were excellent for storage, the ordinary dwelling was usually a single room built from wood, with a fire in the middle (and a hole in the roof above to allow the smoke to escape). This meant storage would mostly be on shelves on the house walls or occasionally in a separate stone-built room outside, using a variety of containers depending on the purpose, such as barrels for pickling or jars for preserved meat sealed with fat. These rooms were later called 'pantries', from the French word for bread, *pain*, and, as domestic buildings developed, they evolved into a room around or off the kitchen, mostly with its own door. The term pantry itself, however, was not in use until the thirteenth century.

A word used slightly earlier was 'larder', which derives

from the Latin for lard. This was a cool place, sometimes built outside the house, and always, whether inside or out, on the north side of the building, with mostly stone floors and shelves. It was used for storing meats and dairy products, with hooks in the ceiling for hanging the meats.

While most food *was* consumed according to the seasons – as we are now being encouraged to do again – our ancestors came up with remarkably ingenious ways of preserving food-stuffs, some of which are still being used by artisan producers today. The traditional processes for this hugely important job included salting, drying (with heat or simply air), smoking, pickling and brining, with a variety of methods for different ingredients.

Many of these processes are extremely old. Pickling using vinegar or brine is a 4,000-year-old method of preservation that protects the body's gut health, helping the body to digest and absorb food. Pickled foods have been keeping people healthy throughout history.

Salting has also been used for thousands of years. Soon after the Romans came to England in AD 43 they started developing saltworks along the east coast. They found an area known by the Celtic name Hellath du (now Cheshire), which had been producing salt for centuries – the earliest evidence dates to 600 BC. Later, Hellath du got the Anglo-Saxon name Northwich, meaning 'northern saltworks'. (The Anglo-Saxons called a saltwork a 'wich', so any place in England with 'wich' at the end at one time produced salt.) Despite this long history, however, salt was expensive to produce, and so smoking meat and fish was often preferred as a cheaper alternative. Salt was still needed for the smoking process, but in much smaller quantities.

Natural fermentation also happened from the earliest times,

offering an easy and natural way to keep and use foods. It was mostly used to produce various forms of alcohol, but also to preserve vegetables and dairy products.

It was the preservation of meat, however – a valuable product – that was particularly important, and it could be extremely effective. Dried meat could keep for years. Various methods were used: pigs, for example, which were reared for meat, were slaughtered in late autumn and then stored in a number of ways. Parts of the animal were salted, smoked, rendered for fat and boiled, and the scraps were used to make meatballs.

Such methods were an indispensable part of Anglo-Saxon life. Not only would preserved foods feed a household throughout a cold and barren winter; they were also necessary lifelines for travellers on land and sea.

Recipes

Barley, Peas and Leeks ✦ Baked Barley
and Mushrooms ✦ Fermented Shredded
Turnip ✦ Horseradish, two ways ✦ Pickled Vegetables:
Cabbage, Fennel and Leeks, Mushrooms, Turnips,
Cucumbers ✦ Sauerkraut ✦ Vinaigrettes ✦ Pease
Pudding ✦ Spiced Walnuts ✦ Dried Fruits
✦ Saxon Rub

Barley, Peas and Leeks

Leeks are not eaten raw but they cook quickly and add a mellow delicious flavour. Do not defrost the frozen peas before cooking – we add them at the end to keep their texture and so they don't get soggy.

- ❖ **200g (7oz) barley**
- ❖ **2 tablespoons chicken fat or olive oil**
- ❖ **2 leeks, sliced**
- ❖ **150g (5oz) frozen peas**
- ❖ **15g (15g) chopped parsley**
- ❖ **Salt and freshly ground black pepper**

Pour 750ml (1¼ pints) water into a saucepan over high heat, add the barley and a large pinch of salt and bring to the boil. Reduce and simmer for 20–25 minutes until the barley is tender. Drain.

Heat the fat in a frying pan over medium heat and cook the leeks until softened, 5–8 minutes. Add salt and pepper and the frozen peas. Stir in the parsley and barley and cook until warmed through. Taste for seasoning before serving.

Baked Barley and Mushrooms

Barley was cultivated around 10,000 years ago, and it has been used both to feed animals and to make bread, beer, soups and stews. When cooked, barley becomes plump and chewy.

The creamy texture in this recipe is a result of adding cheese and butter, which were part of the Saxon diet. Expensive mature cheeses were eaten by the wealthy, while peasants would have had fresh cheese. If you don't happen to have fresh cheese available, substitute it for aged Parmesan. Mace was a spice used in wealthy kitchens along with pepper, ginger, cloves and cinnamon, and was also used to make medicine.

- ❖ 3 tablespoons fat
- ❖ 2 onions, chopped
- ❖ 6 garlic cloves, chopped
- ❖ 450g (1lb) mushrooms, cleaned and quartered, depending on the size
- ❖ 300g (10oz) barley
- ❖ 3 tablespoons grated Parmesan
- ❖ 2 tablespoons butter
- ❖ Large pinch of ground mace
- ❖ Salt and freshly ground black pepper

Preheat the oven to 220°C/425°F/gas 7.

In a heavy-based casserole pot, heat the fat over medium heat and add the onions and garlic, stirring until softened. Add the mushrooms and cook for about 5 minutes until they have softened.

Stir in the barley and 1 litre (1¾ pints) water. Bring to a boil over high heat. Cover the pot and put it in the oven for 30 minutes. The barley will be chewy and most of the water will be gone.

Stir in the Parmesan, butter and mace and season with salt and pepper. Cover the pot and let sit for 15–20 minutes until the rest of the water is absorbed. The barley will become very creamy.

Fermented Shredded Turnip

Fermentation is a good way to preserve turnips, and this method also helps with digestion. Fermentation really plays up the natural sweetness of raw turnip, as well as a bit of that peppery bite that they have. This may simply become your new favourite sauerkraut!

- ❖ **About 1.8kg (4lb) good fresh turnips**
- ❖ **About 120g (4½oz) unrefined sea salt**
- ❖ **Cabbage leaves or cling film**

Shred the turnips with a box or cheese grater into a bowl and sprinkle with the salt all over, coating well. Mix the two together with your hands as the turnips release water for about 5 minutes until you can grab and squeeze the grated turnip and the water releases easily. At this point, transfer the turnip to a non-reactive jar or container that has a lid along with the drained liquid. Tamp down the turnips, releasing any air pockets and ensuring they are entirely submerged. Leave about 5cm (2in) clear at the top of the container.

Place and press and tuck down the cabbage leaves to make sure the mixture stays submerged – how many leaves you need depends on the size and shape of your container. You can also use cling film, pressing down and in. You want to get out any air bubbles and ensure the shredded turnips remain submerged.

Now you can top the container with a fermentation top or lid, which is a wonderful modern convenience, or you can cover the top with a double layer of cheesecloth secured in place with string or an elastic band to keep the contents sanitary and still allow for it to breathe. Check on the contents every so often and scoop out any bits that appear to rot or become mouldy. A fermentation lid will ensure a more hygienic seal, but use your judgement, and remember fermentation lids are rather new!

Fermentation does best in a cool and dark place, and the amount of time it takes depends on temperature – above 20°C (68°F) will take two weeks or so; 18°C (64°F) takes about 3 weeks, while below 15°C (60°F) takes a month or more. To know when it is ready, check the sourness by tasting a little – leave it a bit longer if you want it more sour. When done, seal with a proper lid and store in the fridge or play with extending fermentations! Use before the next growing season.

Horseradish

Horseradish is a pungent and spicy ingredient that was available even in Anglo-Saxon times, possibly brought over by Germanic ancestors. It can be grated and mixed into cultured sour cream or macerated – maceration softens the external wall of the horseradish and draws out its juices.

Grocers stock fresh horseradish, which is a brown-skinned root. If it is dried out, pour 1–2 tablespoons of water into a closed bag with the horseradish and place in the fridge for a few days. The root will draw in the water and reconstitute itself. This same reconstitution process works well with any root vegetable. If fresh horseradish is unavailable, purchase high-quality prepared horseradish, usually found in the refrigerated section of the supermarket.

- ❖ **2 parts freshly grated horseradish**
- ❖ **1 part cultured soured cream**

Simply mix the ingredients together in a bowl and let them come together for an hour. Keeps well for up to a week in a cool place.

To add some extra flavour to your horseradish sauce, add any of the variations listed below.

Simple additions
- ❖ **Chopped fresh dill**
- ❖ **White pepper**
- ❖ **Black pepper**

Marinated Horseradish

* ❖ 2 parts freshly grated horseradish
* ❖ 1 part cider vinegar
* ❖ Honey, to taste
* ❖ Salt

Mix all together in a bowl and marinate for 1 hour or more. Keeps for up to a week in a cold place.

Pickled Cabbage with Apples

Cabbage was probably domesticated in Europe before 1000 BC. It is delicious raw, cooked, fermented (see sauerkraut recipe on page 212) and pickled. The vinegar and salt used in the pickling process 'cure' the cabbage.

The first mention of apples in England was by King Alfred in about AD 885 in his English translation of Pope Gregory's *Pastoral Care*.

- ❖ 500g (1lb 2oz) green cabbage, finely shredded
- ❖ 140g (5oz) salt
- ❖ 500ml (18fl oz) cider vinegar
- ❖ 200ml (7fl oz) white wine
- ❖ 300g (10oz) honey
- ❖ 2 teaspoons black peppercorns
- ❖ 6 bay leaves
- ❖ 2 tablespoons mustard seeds
- ❖ 1 Pink Lady apple, peeled, cored and thinly sliced lengthways

Place the shredded cabbage in a colander in the sink and sprinkle all over with salt, mixing well. Leave for 2 hours. Wash the cabbage with cold water until the salt washes away.

Meanwhile, put the vinegar, wine, honey, peppercorns and bay leaves into a saucepan and simmer until the liquid has reduced by half, 20–30 minutes. Set aside to infuse and come to room temperature.

Strain through a sieve into a bowl, discarding the peppercorns and bay leaves. Put the cabbage, mustard seeds and apple into a bowl and pour over the strained liquid. Transfer the cabbage and liquid to jars, seal and store in a cold place for up to a month.

Pickled Fennel and Leeks

Fennel was used as food and medicine in ancient Egypt. Leeks were one of the most popular vegetables eaten by the Anglo-Saxons.

- ❖ **2 fennel bulbs**
- ❖ **2 leeks**
- ❖ **2 tablespoons salt**
- ❖ **500ml (18fl oz) cider vinegar**
- ❖ **250g (9oz) honey**
- ❖ **2 teaspoons mustard seeds**

Remove the top part of the fennel. Halve the bulb and cut into thin slices. Wash the slices. Trim the root end and cut off the leeks where the pale green turns to dark green. Halve the white and pale green part lengthwise and wash, checking for dirt between the layers of leaves.

Combine the fennel and leeks in a bowl. Add the salt and toss to evenly coat. Add cold water to cover, then stir to dissolve the salt. Set aside for 1 hour, then taste and feel the fennel. It should be slightly softened. Drain.

Meanwhile, combine the vinegar, honey and mustard seeds in a saucepan and simmer for 5 minutes over medium heat. Set aside to cool.

Divide the fennel and leeks equally among containers with lids and pour the brine over to completely cover. Seal tightly and place in a cold place for a day to allow the flavours to permeate the fennel. The pickles will keep for at least a month in a cold place.

Pickled Mushrooms

Slightly sweet with honey and brightened with herbs, these mushrooms have a complexity of flavour that makes them useful as a snack, side or condiment.

- ❖ **60ml (2½fl oz) cider vinegar**
- ❖ **4–5 garlic cloves**
- ❖ **A few sprigs of thyme or marjoram**
- ❖ **1 tablespoon honey**
- ❖ **Pinch of freshly ground black pepper**
- ❖ **1–2 teaspoons coarse salt**
- ❖ **450g (1lb) mixed mushrooms, such as oysters, enokis, cremini, and shiitakes, cleaned with kitchen paper**

Combine the vinegar, garlic, thyme or marjoram, honey, pepper and salt in a pan and bring to the boil over medium heat. Add the mushrooms (larger ones first since they take longer to cook) and cook for a few minutes, until the mushrooms are all tender. Take the pan off the heat and leave the mushrooms to cool in the liquid.

Once cool, transfer the mushrooms and their cooking liquid to clean mason jars. Seal tightly and place in a cold place, where they will keep for at least a month.

Pickled Turnips

- ❖ **750ml (1¼ pints) water**
- ❖ **70g (3oz) coarse salt**
- ❖ **1 bay leaf**
- ❖ **250ml (8fl oz) white vinegar**
- ❖ **900g (2lb) turnips, peeled**
- ❖ **1 garlic clove, peeled**

Heat one-third of the water in a large pan over medium heat. Add the salt and bay leaf, stirring until the salt is dissolved. Remove from the heat and let cool to room temperature. Once cool, add the vinegar and the rest of the water, stirring to combine.

Cut the turnips into batons, about the size of thick French fries. Put the turnips and garlic into a clean jar, then pour the salted brine over them, including the bay leaf. Cover and let sit at room temperature, in a cool place, for one week – they will mellow after a few days. The pickles will keep for a month in a cold place.

Pickled Cucumbers

Cleopatra attributed some of her beauty to pickles; Aristotle praised the healing effects of pickled cucumbers; and later peoples also highly valued pickled cucumbers.

Dill, one of the most important herbs used in pickling cucumbers and other vegetables, arrived in Western Europe from its native Sumatra around AD 900, although ancient Greeks and Romans used it extensively centuries earlier.

- ❖ 120ml (4fl oz) vinegar
- ❖ 120ml (4fl oz) water
- ❖ 1 teaspoon salt
- ❖ 1 tablespoon honey
- ❖ 2 cucumbers, rinsed and thickly sliced
- ❖ 1 tablespoon dill leaves
- ❖ 1 teaspoon caraway seeds

Combine the vinegar, water, salt and honey in a saucepan and heat until the honey has dissolved.

Place the cucumbers in a bowl and pour the vinegar and honey mix over them. Sprinkle in the dill and caraway seeds. Leave for 2 hours before eating.

The cucumber slices will keep in the pickling liquid stored in a cold place for about a week.

Sauerkraut

Fermentation is a natural way to preserve and stabilise foods, but you need to exercise a little caution with this process. This is a controlled rot of sorts, but a good rule of thumb is that if it smells good and appetising, you are fine. Fermentation has been done for centuries and in less-clean areas than the modern and maintained kitchen, but you still should be vigilant about your preparations and keep everything clean at all times, washing and sanitising your workspace and equipment. Soap and water are fine, as are natural cleaners, but don't use bleach.

- ❖ **1 head of cabbage, about 1.8kg (4lb) total**
- ❖ **95g (3½oz) unrefined sea salt**

Shred the cabbage with a knife or mandolin, reserving a couple of leaves, and sprinkle all over with the salt. Mix everything together well with your hands to help the cabbage release water, reserving the liquid. This should take about 5 minutes, until you can grab and squeeze the grated cabbage and the water releases easily. At this point, transfer the cabbage to a non-reactive jar or container that has a lid along with the drained liquid. Tamp down the cabbage, releasing any air pockets and ensuring everything is entirely submerged. Leave about 5cm (2in) clear at the top of the container.

Tuck down the reserved cabbage leaves on top of the shredded mix to make sure the mixture stays submerged. You can also use cling film, pressing down and in. You want to get out any air bubbles and ensure the shredded cabbage remains submerged.

As with the recipe for Fermented Shredded Turnip (see recipe on page 202) now you can top the container with a fermentation top or lid, or you can cover the top with a double layer of cheesecloth secured in place with string or an elastic band to keep the contents sanitary and still allow for it to breathe. Check on the contents every so often and scoop out any bits that appear to rot or become mouldy. A fermentation lid will ensure a more hygienic seal.

Fermentation does best in a cool and dark place, and the amount of time it takes depends on temperature; above 20°C (68°F) will take 2 weeks or so; 18°C (64°F) takes about 3 weeks, while below 15°C (60°F) takes a month or more. To know when it is ready, check the sourness by tasting a little – leave it a bit longer if you want it more sour. When done, seal with a proper lid and store in the fridge or play with extending fermentations! Use before the next growing season.

Vinaigrettes

Vinegar is mentioned in the Bible and its history of usage goes back 10,000 years. The Egyptians, Babylonians and Persians all used it to preserve food. It was the Romans who brought cider vinegar to the Saxons. Vinegar was and still is very versatile – it was used for pickling and marinating beef, was added to whey (residue from soft cheese making) to make more cheese, and it was mixed with honey and herbs to make a sauce. The Anglo-Saxons made salads with a large variety of green leaves and seasoned them with garlic, oil, vinegar and salt. In the early spring, a salad might have included shoots sprouting from root vegetables stored in cellars.

Here are three vinaigrettes that use ingredients that were available to Anglo-Saxons.

Juniper Vinaigrette

We are taking a little leeway here on ingredients, but we do know that juniper berries and walnuts are both ancient, having been in existence for thousands of years – the Romans used juniper berries as a cheaper substitute for black peppercorns.

The predominate flavour of gin is juniper berries, so for the deliciousness of juniper vinaigrette, we are using gin. The earliest-known reference to gin was in the thirteenth century, so it must have been around for a while, right?

Shallots were introduced into Europe by the crusaders in the eleventh century and are available in most supermarkets, but if you can't get hold of them, you can use onion instead.

- ❖ 1 tablespoon juniper berries
- ❖ 1 shallot
- ❖ 2 tablespoons cider or white vinegar
- ❖ 1 tablespoon gin
- ❖ 2 tablespoons olive oil
- ❖ 2 tablespoons walnut oil
- ❖ 1 tablespoon boiling water
- ❖ Bunch of chives
- ❖ Salt and freshly ground black pepper

Combine all the ingredients except the water and chives in a blender. Process for 30 seconds. With the motor running add the water and pulse. Stir in the chives.

Transfer to a jar with a lid and store in a cold place for up to one week.

Chicken Fat Vinaigrette

- ❖ 3 tablespoons chicken fat
- ❖ 1 tablespoon apple cider vinegar
- ❖ 1–2 teaspoons dried thyme or chervil, or fennel seeds
- ❖ Salt and freshly ground black pepper

Put the chicken fat into a pan and warm over low heat. Whisk the cider vinegar and 1 tablespoon of boiling water into the hot fat, or process in a small blender for 30 seconds. Add the herbs and salt and pepper to taste.

Transfer to a jar with a lid and store in a cold place for up to one week.

Bacon Fat Vinaigrette

- ❖ 3 tablespoons bacon fat
- ❖ 1 tablespoon each vinegar and mustard
- ❖ Salt and freshly ground black pepper

Pour the bacon fat into a pan and warm over low heat. Whisk the vinegar and mustard into the hot fat, or process in a small blender for 30 seconds. Add salt and pepper to taste.

Transfer to a jar with a lid and store in a cold place for up to one week.

Pease Pudding

Pease pudding is one of the oldest of English dishes. Dried split peas, easy to store, were an important protein in Anglo-Saxon recipes, and carrot and mint have been mentioned in contemporary texts – we know that herbs were an essential part of Anglo-Saxon life, not just for cooking but for medicinal purposes, too.

- ❖ **200g (7oz) dried yellow split peas**
- ❖ **1 onion, cut in half**
- ❖ **1 carrot, roughly chopped into large chunks**
- ❖ **1 tablespoon butter**
- ❖ **Handful of mint leaves, chopped (optional)**

Soak the split peas overnight in a bowl of water. Drain.

Tip the drained split peas into a saucepan, then add the onion halves and carrot chunks. Add enough water to cover, bring to a boil over high heat, then reduce the heat and simmer for an hour or so until the peas are tender.

Drain the peas and remove the onion and carrot chunks. Return the peas to the pan and mush them with a wooden spoon or use a modern-day blender. Stir in the butter and mint, if using.

Spiced Walnuts

A recipe using what was available to the Anglo-Saxons from walnut and hazelnut trees. They may have not made spiced nuts, but this recipe is too good not to include. The Saxons' food was more sophisticated than we think; similar to contemporary diners, they would eat one meat and two vegetable meals each day, serving their meat with fruit sauces, clarified butter, whipped cream and salted vegetables. The wealthy hosted feasts, so it's not difficult to imagine that a dish of spiced nuts might have found its way onto the Saxon table.

Mace is an important element here; it was a spice that was used only in wealthy kitchens to flavour food, along with pepper, ginger, cloves and cinnamon.

- ¾ teaspoon each ground mace, cinnamon and ginger
- ¼ teaspoon grated nutmeg
- 2 teaspoons freshly cracked black pepper
- 1 teaspoon salt
- 170g (6oz) honey
- 1 egg white
- 350g (12oz) walnuts or hazelnuts, roughly chopped into large chunks

Preheat the oven to 170°C/325°F/gas 3.

Stir the spices and seasoning together in a bowl and mix in the honey.

Whisk the egg white in a clean bowl until barely frothy. Add the nuts to the egg white, then pour in the honey and spices and stir to coat.

Spread on a baking sheet and cook for about 1 hour until golden.

Dried Fruits

Drying was the earliest form of food preservation. Large areas were covered with hardwood trees and berry-bearing bushes. Apples, crab apples, pears, cherries, strawberries and blackberries were available in summer and autumn, and when they fell to the ground they dried in the sun. When dried, these fruits were valued for their sweetness and long shelf life.

These fruits can be air-dried or baked in a low-temperature oven until firm, slightly chewy and shrivelled around the edges. If you like, you can add honey to taste.

- ❖ **2–3 pears, such as Comice or Williams, or apples, or use strawberries, blackberries or cherries**
- ❖ **Sugar or honey, to taste (optional)**

Preheat the oven to 110°C/225°F/gas ¼. Line a baking sheet with baking parchment.

Cut the pears or apples into slices lengthwise, about 3mm (⅛in) thick. Spread a little honey on each slice, if using. Strawberries and blackberries can be left whole or thickly sliced, make sure cherries have been pitted before baking. Make sure the fruits are thoroughly dry before drizzling with honey.

Cook in the oven until the fruits are dry, about 3 or more hours – they will be shrivelled, chewy and firmer.

Transfer to an airtight container and store in a cool, dry place; they will keep for up to 6 weeks.

Saxon Rub

A rub is a combination of spices, peppers and salts that are used for seasoning meats before cooking to enhance flavour and texture. These spices, especially peppercorns, would have been luxury items, but fennel, coriander, savory and other herbs would have been available to those able to forage and farm. Feel free to try others such as mint, thyme or oregano, but always use them dried. Steer clear of parsley, which the Saxons considered a poisonous flirtation with Satan.

- ❖ 1 tablespoon fennel seeds
- ❖ 1 tablespoon coriander seeds
- ❖ 1 tablespoon white peppercorns
- ❖ 1 tablespoon black peppercorns
- ❖ 1 tablespoon dried savory

Combine all the ingredients using a pestle and mortar (ideally) or a spice grinder – the mortar and pestle allows one to feel the work and effort needed to transform the spices, connecting one more to the practice. Grind the combined ingredients to your preferred texture – coarse or fine.

Store in an airtight container in a cool, dry place. Use while still pungent, within six months.

THE LAST SHIELD WALL

Storing and preserving food was vital to long sea voyages, and even after Uhtred has achieved his life's ambition, regained Bebbanburg and found himself living in a country called Englaland, he still needs to sail into battle. He might be older, but he has never lost his warrior spirit . . .

'She's called the *Seafang*,' Gerbruht said flatly, 'out of the Tinan.'

We were standing on the rock terrace just outside Bebbanburg's great hall, gazing at a ship coming northwards.

'Big boat,' I said. 'Cargo?'

'Offshore fishing,' Gerbruht said, sounding sullen.

'Who owns her?' Finan asked lazily.

'Twicca Leofson,' Gerbruht said unhappily.

'Ah,' Finan sounded more lively. 'He married the priest's daughter!'

'Which priest?' I asked.

'The fat daughter,' Finan added at the same time.

'She wasn't fat,' Gerbruht insisted.

'Father Ælfric,' Finan said, 'he has a church on the Tinan's north bank. Poor bugger had six daughters and the fat one was the last he got rid of. Christ's bones, but that girl must have cost a fortune to feed!'

'She was not fat!' Gerbruht insisted.

'Can't remember her name,' Finan said. 'Olla?'

'Ella,' Gerbruht said, unhappy still.

'And this Frisian idiot,' Finan jerked a thumb towards Gerbruht, 'was sweet on fat Ella. Good God, man,' he was talking to Gerbruht now, 'she was so fat a cripple could have caught her and you let her get away!'

225

'She was not fat,' Gerbruht said yet again. 'Sturdy, maybe.'

'Sturdy!' Finan retorted. 'She's big enough to stand in the shield wall!'

He turned and looked south. Finan, bored with teasing him, had also turned and was looking towards the ship that was heading inshore of the Farnea Islands.

'The bastard is coming here,' he said disapprovingly.

The *Seafang* looked to be a fine ship and was making good speed on a brisk east wind. She was broad in the beam, but had a proud cutwater crowned with a wooden cross. Her main deck was thronged with people.

'Could be going to Lindisfarena,' I said. 'Pilgrims, perhaps?'

'No one goes there any more,' Finan said. 'And if they walked as far as the Tinan why take a ship for the last few miles?'

'They're coming here,' Gerbruht said firmly, and I believed him. He was the best seaman among my men; a big strong Frisian who had grown up with boats and could helm as well as he could fight. 'She's too close inshore,' Gerbruht explained, 'and he's fighting the tide.' A spray of white foam shattered from the *Seafang*'s bow. 'If he was going to Lindisfarena he would have gone outside the islands to avoid the worst of the current. Twicca Leofson may be a worthless bastard, but he knows this coast.'

'Twenty, thirty people on board,' Finan said. 'Probably means trouble.'

We watched for a few more minutes, seeing the big sail drop as the ship passed the northern end of Bebbanburg, and then she turned into our shallow harbour entrance and a dozen oars were thrust out to carry her safe into the channel. 'Go and see what they want,' I told Gerbruht.

'And be nice to Twicca!' Finan called after him.

'You should be nice to Gerbruht,' I chided Finan, 'he's a good man.'

'He is! But he's slow. That girl was monstrous, big as a bullock! And all Gerbruht did was make sheep eyes at her. If he'd given that girl a loaf of bread and a goose leg she'd have been flat on her back in an eyeblink, but Gerbruht just sighed to her.'

'Poor Gerbruht,' I said.

'And it's trouble,' Finan warned me. 'Folk don't come here unless they need help.'

'And we give it when we can.'

I went into the great hall where, moments later, a boy ran in. 'There are twenty-six people coming, lord,' he told me.

'Happy people?' Finan demanded.

'The women were crying, lord.' The boy had been sent by Gerbruht to warn me.

'Told you it was trouble,' Finan said, 'and they'll want feeding. Pray Twicca didn't bring his wife.'

'You are an evil man,' I told him, then turned as Benedetta came from the back chambers.

'There are people coming to see you,' she said. 'I saw them.' She had brought a heavy woollen cloak which she insisted I wear. 'You must look like a king.'

'It's too warm for a cloak!' I protested.

'Then suffer,' she said, draping the cloak around my shoulders and fixing it with a golden brooch at my neck.

'Besides,' I grumbled, 'I'm not a king.'

'You are greater than any king in Britain,' she insisted, 'you are Uhtred of Bebbanburg.' She tugged the cloak's collar then gave me a kiss. 'Be nice to your people. They will want food?'

'Give them the stale bread and hard cheese,' I suggested. 'Tell them the king's storerooms are empty.'

'*Ouff*,' she said, her universal sound of disapproval. 'We will feed them!' She vanished to tyrannise the kitchens and Finan and I waited until a babble of voices told me our visitors had arrived. They filed through the hall door, accompanied by a score of my men who were simply curious to discover why the *Seafang* had sailed to us.

I watched the crowd approach until they filled the space between the big central hearth and the dais where I sat. The women were indeed crying, the men looked stern. There was a priest with them and I assumed he would be their spokes-man, but instead a tall, well-built man with a short-sword at his waist instructed them to kneel.

'Lord,' he greeted me from his knees.

'Stand up,' I told him, 'and tell me who you are.'

'I am Twicca Leofson, lord, and I live on your land.'

'You're welcome, Twicca Leofson,' I said, 'and why are you here?'

That question provoked a score of voices, all speaking at once, while the women cried even louder.

'Enough!' I shouted. 'One man speaks for you all.' I nodded at Twicca. 'You. Talk to me.'

He spoke, and spoke well, though the story he told was miserable. It had happened the day before our meeting and Twicca recounted how he had taken *Seafang* far offshore to the shallow banks of the North Sea where the fishing was good. He returned to the Tinan just after dawn and saw four ships sailing eastwards. He thought nothing of it. 'They looked Frisian, lord,' he explained, 'and there's plenty of Frisians trade in the Tinan.'

'Go on,' I encouraged him.

'And they were traders, lord. Slavers.' He spat the last word, then went on to tell me how he had found their village devastated. The ships had come in the night and their crews had rounded up all the young children and women. 'Fifty-eight in all, lord,' he said, 'most of them youngsters. They killed eighteen men.'

'Frisians,' I said.

'They were, lord!' the priest spoke for the first time. 'I heard them talking, lord, and their speech is like ours.'

'Like enough,' I agreed. 'And you are?'

'Father Ælfric, lord,' he said, 'we met when . . .'

'I remember,' I said, though I had absolutely no memory of meeting him. 'You're sure they weren't Danes?'

'They were Frisian,' Twicca insisted. 'Their ships were Frisian.' He would know a Frisian vessel from a Danish one. They were similar, of course, but a Frisian ship tended to be flatter amidships, which not everyone liked, though all admitted no one built ships as fine as the Frisians. My own ship, *Spearhafoc*, was Frisian built and she was a marvel.

'How many in their crews?' I asked.

The priest again answered. 'I counted more than a hundred men, lord. Most of them in mail.'

I frowned. Four ships? I doubted any of the four would have less than forty men in its crew which suggested the Frisians had numbered at least a hundred and fifty. I saw that the priest had a blood-scabbed bruise on his forehead. 'You fought them, Father?'

'I tried,' the old man said. 'They stole the sacrament from the church!' A woman wailed, and the priest hurried on, 'Stole the altar vessels, lord. Everything!'

'They took my wife and children, lord,' Twicca said.

'Your wife is Ella, yes?' I asked.

'She is, lord!' Twicca sounded amazed that I knew his wife's name.

'Then we must get Ella and the others back,' I said, and looked over their heads to Gerbruht. 'How long before *Spearhafoc* is ready?'

'She'll be afloat tonight, lord,' Gerbruht said. I had ordered the ship hauled onto the hard where we had dug burn-pits to make pitch and were now caulking her seams after a long summer. 'Just needs time for the seams to settle.'

'Then we sail tomorrow,' I said, 'a full crew and war gear. And you,' I pointed at Twicca, 'will come with us.'

'Of course, lord,' he said, and I saw Gerbruht shudder. He looked as if he was about to protest, but I ignored him, turning to Benedetta instead. 'We'll need supplies.'

She nodded grimly. Like me she abhorred slavery. She had been a slave herself, snatched from her Italian home as a child and brought to Britain where she had been a slave till I freed her. And I too had pulled an oar with an iron collar chafing my neck and with manacles on my feet, and ever since I had treated slavers as enemies. Now slavers had dared come to my coast and had taken my people. So *Spearhafoc* must sail to war.

'And how do we find them?' Finan asked me that night. 'As I remember there's a long coast in Frisia.'

'Long and treacherous,' I said, 'but they must be found.'

I had sent Berg Skallagrimmrson north to the Tuede to summon his brother, Egil, which meant we would travel to Frisia in two ships, both with full crews of warriors. My ship, *Spearhafoc*, would hold my men, while Egil's Danes would crew *Banamaðr*. And God help the Frisians who had come to the Tinan, I thought, when we led those hardened warriors ashore. Though the slavers would be hard to find. The Frisian shore is a tangle of islands, sandbanks, creeks, rivers and marshlands. It was an easy place to go aground, and a difficult place to approach a village unseen, and there were hundreds of miles of that desolate wetland, and I did not doubt that the slavers would half expect our coming. From what the priest had told me it sounded as if upwards of one hundred and fifty men.

'They'll hold the captives hostage,' Finan suggested gloomily, 'start killing them if we get too close.'

'Like as not,' I said.

'Why bother?' Finan asked.

'Some bastard from Frisia raids my land,' I said, 'means I have to repay him.'

'I thought you were supposed to ask the king's help.'

'Bugger the king,' I growled. 'By the time I've sent a messenger to Wintanceaster and his reply has reached me a month will have passed. And all he'll tell me to do is wait while he sends a priest to talk to the Frisians, and what use will that be? Better for us to punish the Frisian bastard.'

The king was Æthelstan who, ever since the mighty battle at Brunanburh had been known as the King of all Englaland. I liked Æthelstan, but he had let it be known that any attack on his land, and Bebbanburg was now undoubtedly a part of Englaland, should be reported to him and he would decide on the appropriate response, and I did not doubt that his initial reaction, far from telling me to sail across the sea and break a few heads, would be to order a priest to make the voyage and talk peace to the attackers. Æthelstan had become almost as pious as his grandfather, Alfred, and I knew that if he did indeed send a priest then the poor man, if he could even find the attackers, would not survive the mission.

'You shouldn't go,' Benedetta told me that same night.

'And why not?'

'You are an old man.'

'Who leads the wolves of Bebbanburg,' I said, 'and they are young men. I'm going.'

'You told me that Brunanburh,' she had trouble pronouncing the name, 'would be your last fight!'

'This won't be a fight,' I said, 'it'll be a massacre. And tell the kitchens to put food and ale on board *Spearhafoc*, enough for fifty men for two weeks.'

'Two weeks?'

'It won't take that long,' I said, though I suspected it might last longer, but two weeks was a reasonable guess. I had sailed to Frisia many times and knew the journey would be up to three days each way and reckoned my business there should not last longer than a week.

'You are a fool,' Benedetta said, though not unkindly, 'you only go because you like a fight.'

'So do you,' I retorted, 'want to come?'

'Two weeks on a ship? *Ouff!* I stay here. And you,' she said as she turned towards the kitchens, 'let your young men do the fighting! Not you!'

Next morning Benedetta told me she had sent three barrels of ale and three of food down to the ship. 'Bread, smoked herring and salt pork,' she said.

'No vegetables?'

'You'll only throw them overboard,' she said, which was true enough, and a half-hour later we saw *Banamaðr* coming fast, riding ahead of a brisk north wind.

'Let's not waste time!' I said and hurried out of the Skull Gate with my fifty warriors. I said goodbye to Benedetta at the gate, assuring her I would return, then followed my men around the harbour's edge. A half-dozen shabby barrels sat on the sand beside *Spearhafoc* and I shouted at my men to stow them on board, then we heaved the ship down the log rollers and clambered aboard.

Gerbruht had already checked the ship and declared her ready for sea and, hoping to meet Egil before he negotiated the narrow harbour entrance, I ordered the big sail hoisted up the mast, then sheeted in so that *Spearhafoc* caught the wind and sped across the small harbour.

'Showing off?' Finan asked, amused.

'I'm making a show,' I grunted. We almost always rowed out of the harbour. It was slower, but much safer because the entrance channel was perilously narrow and subject to shoaling, but *Spearhafoc* and I were going to war and we would go in style. The wind was pushing her fast, the sail was bellying out, resplendent with the wolf's head of Bebbanburg, and her wake was white and spreading. I heaved on the steering-oar to take her into the channel. If she struck sand then it would be an ignominious end to my flaunting departure, but I kept her in the channel's centre and heard men cheering from the ramparts above the Sea Gate. The wake broke in waves either side of the channel as we sped through and then *Spearhafoc* trembled as her bows met the first breaking sea.

We were free of the land and I let out a whoop of triumph as we left the beach and fortress behind. 'A fast trip and a slaughter when we get there,' I said to Finan.

'If we ever find the earsling.'

'We'll find him.'

I called to Twicca, the fisherman, who was sitting on one of the rowers' benches. 'You've sailed to Frisia?' I asked.

'A score of times, lord,'

'Then take the oar,' I said, and let him grip the steering-oar as I worked my way forward to the high bow where a great beaked bird-head stood atop the cutwater. *Banamaðr* had already turned eastwards, but she was a smaller ship than *Spearhafoc* and we quickly closed on her. 'Take me close!' I called to Twicca, then had my crew brail up the lower part of the mainsail to lessen our speed as we drew alongside Egil's ship.

Egil Skallagrimmrson was like a brother to me. He was a Dane, a poet, a pagan, a seaman and a warrior. He lived on the southern bank of the Tuede where I had given him a swathe of land that was now the northern border of King Æthelstan's Englaland, which meant that any Scots coming south to take my cattle first had to get past Egil. Few did, and those few usually did not live long enough to regret it. He had fought beside me at Brunanburh and in a dozen other battles and, other than Finan, there was no man I would rather have as a battle-companion. Now he bellowed a greeting across the water, 'So! An enemy in Frisia? How many?'

'At least four boat crews,' I said, gesturing at my own ship to suggest crews the same size as mine.

'Let's hope there are more! You know where they are?'

'No.' I grabbed the ship's side as a great wave tipped *Spearhafoc* and lurched her towards *Banamaðr*. Egil steered away from us and laughed because I had almost fallen into the sea.

'We'll find them!' he shouted. 'With or without you!'

'We'll kill them,' I answered.

'What else?' He laughed. 'I was beginning to get bored!'

'You could always declare war on the Scots?' I suggested.

'Too easy. Maybe I'll capture all Englaland. Saxon women!'

'You don't have enough already?'

'A man can never have enough of women, ale or enemies!' He waved and leaned on his steering-oar to swerve *Banamaðr* away from *Spearhafoc* again. My sail had stolen much of the wind from Egil's ship and *Banamaðr* had not responded to the oar, but instead veered towards us. Twicca should have steered away, but when I turned to shout at him I saw him struggling with Gerbruht for the steering-oar's loom.

'Stop it!' I bellowed and hurried aft. 'What are you doing?'

'The bastard nearly stove us in!' Gerbruht snarled. 'He shouldn't be steersman.'

'It was a wave,' I said, 'let go of him.'

In truth Gerbruht was the better sailor, but he had not taken a ship to Frisia nearly as often as Twicca, and Twicca had the fisherman's knowledge of the sea. He could read the waves, the sky, and the night's stars, and I did not doubt he would take us where we wished to go.

He had no chance to see the stars that night because the sky was covered in thick cloud, but the wind stayed to the north; a cold wind bringing squalls of rain that drummed on the sail and dripped on the men trying to shelter below. I stayed on the steering platform, swathed in a great cloak, and let Twicca drive the ship on. 'Over the banks now,' he grunted once.

'You're sure?'

'Feel the waves, lord. They're shorter. They'll drop off soon. We're making good time.'

I fed the men that night, opening a cask of bread that also contained some blocks of hard cheese. We drank ale and some time after that meal I fell asleep.

I woke to a grey stormy dawn. The seas were bigger, their tops whipped to white by the risen wind. Gerbruht had taken the steering-oar from Twicca who was sleeping down among the rowers' benches. 'How's she running?' I asked him.

'Like a bird,' Gerbruht said happily.

'And *Banamaðr*?'

'Behind us, lord.'

I looked aft and saw Egil's serpent-ship climbing a wave then falling into the trough with a great spray of white foam. 'Don't get too far ahead,' I said.

'We'll shorten sail, lord. Pity to slow her, though.'

'A bigger pity to fight an enemy without Egil,' I retorted.

We shortened sail, though it still took Egil all morning to catch us. It was a good morning. The wind had dropped and the seas settled and *Spearhafoc* cut her way smoothly eastwards. I stayed at the stern, simply enjoying the day. Finan and Benedetta might dislike the sea, but for me it has always been a joy; to feel the ship quiver to the beat of waves, to surge under the wind, to enjoy the freedom of a good ship seething under the sun. Finan, ever suspicious of the sea and ships, brought me a pot of ale. 'Drink it slowly,' he said, 'there's not much left.'

'There should be three casks!'

'There's one,' he said bluntly. 'One of ale and one of bread with some cheese.'

I nodded forward. 'I can see six.'

'Aye, you can, but guess what's in four of them.'

'Vegetables?' I suggested in disgust.

'Pitch.'

'Pitch?'

'Solid blocks of bloody pitch. They put the wrong barrels on board.'

I went forward to check for myself, but Finan was right. *Spearhafoc* had been hauled ashore to have her seams caulked, and so much pitch had been burned out of the pine logs that there had been a surplus, which, once it had cooled, had been knocked into lumps and stored in barrels. The lumps could be reheated over a fire to caulk another ship, which was a lot

236

faster than leeching pine in a fire-pit to make new pitch, but the stored pitch barrels had, in our haste, been loaded aboard.

'We'll be chewing pitch by tomorrow,' Finan said darkly.

'We'll be in Frisia by tomorrow,' I said, 'we'll get food there.'

'And that thin ale they make? No better than horse piss.'

I slapped him on the shoulder. 'Cheer up! We'll take what we need even if it is horse piss!'

Finan might have been downcast, but I was in heaven. I stood at the prow for a time, just gazing at the ship and marvelling, as I always did, at how this man-made assemblage of linen, hemp and wood came together so perfectly. The wind filled the sail, the mast and the stays creaked under the strain, and water hissed down the hull and curled cream in our wake. She was a beautiful ship, *Spearhafoc*, and I patted her timbers as if to thank her for looking after us.

Twicca came forward and tugged at his forelock in greeting. 'Wind's backing, lord.'

'That'll help,' I said cheerfully.

'Might,' he allowed, 'but like as not we'll sail into fog.'

'Then they won't see us coming!'

'And we won't know where we're going,' he grunted. He looked at the sea. 'Still a way to go yet, lord.'

'Maybe tonight?'

'Maybe. Current's still helping us. When it sets us southwards, lord, we'll know we're closing on the coast.' I wondered how he could tell, but did not ask. He had far more sea miles under his belt than I did. He scowled. 'You might want to tell that Frisian lump to steer a wee bit northwards?'

'Gerbruht,' I said, 'is probably as good a seaman as you, and he knows the Frisian coast. How come you know it?'

'You catch a good haul of fish on the banks, lord, and along comes a nasty westerly. Best thing to do is ride it to Frisia, sell the catch, then head back and fish again. The bastards cheat you, of course, but it's all money.'

'And their ale?' I asked.

'Bilge water, lord. My dogs piss better ale than they make.'

'Have the rest of that,' I said, giving him the pot Finan had brought me, 'it's good Bebbanburg ale. And don't worry, Twicca, we'll fetch your wife back.'

'And the children,' he said, then nodded. 'Thank you, lord.' He took the ale aft and sat disconsolate on a rower's bench.

Twicca was proved right as a fog followed the wind's turning. I could see the fogbank creeping from behind, then it engulfed us and the temperature dropped. The wind kept steady, blowing us now directly towards the Frisian coast, and *Spearhafoc* slid through a grey world. Egil's ship was just visible to the south of us as a dark, lean shadow. Egil was steering her, standing tall at the sternpost and peering intently forward. Neither of us slowed. We could have been sailing into the underworld, but Twicca was certain we were still safely offshore. I was nervous and I was sure Egil shared my fears, but neither of us shortened sail even when the fog darkened as the sun faded behind us. I too peered ahead, hoping for a glimpse of waves breaking on a beach or, if I was lucky, the glow of a fire in one of the settlements built atop a sandbank. I saw nothing.

Egil had a man in the bows throwing a stone-weighted line into the sea. The line had knots tied at regular intervals and some time after dark I heard a hoarse shout and a moment later sensed *Banamaðr* coming closer.

'Time to anchor!' Egil shouted. 'And hope the tide's low!'

We both anchored. Then we slept.

*   *   *

I slept badly, woken from time to time whenever a gust of wind tugged *Spearhafoc* and she was brought up with a jerk against the anchor's line. Those gusts became less frequent and the wind was almost calm when I was woken by Finan.

'We're there,' he grunted, 'wherever that is.'

I groaned, feeling the ache in my joints, then sat up to see that we were close to a sandy shore, or rather to great sand dunes rearing from a wave-fretted beach. The fog had thinned and nothing else was visible, only sand and, not far away *Banamaðr* held by her anchor line.

'Here,' Finan said, handing me a pot of ale, 'from the dregs, and there's cold pitch for breakfast.'

I went forward and peered through the thinning fog and saw into what I called the Inner Sea that lay beyond the big dunes. I knew the Frisians called it the Waadsee, but my father had always talked disparagingly of the 'mud-folk' who lived on the Inner Sea, and the name had stuck with me.

'Tide's rising, lord.' Twicca had joined me. 'If you want to go inside, now's a good time. Current's with us.'

'Now's a good time,' I responded. 'Did you get anything to eat?'

'A little, lord.'

There was no point in trying to sail into the Inner Sea, so we hauled the anchor stone and put the long oars into their tholes.

'Row!' Gerbruht shouted from the steering-oar and, slowly at first, *Spearhafoc* headed towards the gap in the great sand-banks. I remembered the last fight I had endured in these strange waters. I had brought *Seolferwulf*, another good ship, and killed Skirnir and his savages on a bare sand island. It had not been a fight, it had been a massacre, and I supposed Skirnir's bones still lay on that barren heap of sand.

239

'Do you know where we are?' I asked Twicca, who still stood beside me at the prow.

'Frisia, lord,' he said, and said no more.

Spearhafoc shuddered as her elmwood keel scraped on sand, but Gerbruht bellowed at the oarsmen, they heaved, and we slid over the shoal and found deeper water again. *Banamaðr* was following us, but she was a shallower ship than *Spearhafoc* and crossed the sandbar without touching bottom.

'Ship ahead, lord,' Twicca said, and I turned to gaze east again and saw a small boat, almost certainly a fishing boat, some way ahead. She was an indistinct shape in the mist and using the small wind to head out towards us, but even as I saw her the sail dropped, she put out oars and turned to flee inshore.

'So they know we're coming, lord,' Twicca said unhappily.

'Whoever they are.'

'They'll think we're trouble.'

'We are, Twicca,' I said, 'we're more than trouble, we're a nightmare.' I cupped my hands. 'Hoist the sail!'

'Lord,' Twicca said nervously.

'I need speed,' I said curtly. He was worried about going aground, but I had sailed the Inner Sea often enough to know it was mostly deep water and it was only when we reached the further shore that the shoals would threaten us.

The wind caught the great sail and *Spearhafoc* creaked as she leaned to the breeze and the water hurried down her lean flanks.

'We'll need the oars soon!' I told my men to stop them stowing them in the ship's centre, then leaned on the steering-oar to head slightly off the wind. Egil had hoisted his great eagle sail and *Banamaðr* seethed up from astern, the water foaming white at her cutwater. Egil, standing at the stern, bellowed across the water to me, 'You're following that poor fellow?'

'Yes!'

'She'll lead you into shallow water!'

'Probably!'

That was what I would have done in the fisherman's place. I would have taken my small boat into a creek where we could not follow. I was certain he had dropped his sail because he was heading for just such a place where it was safer to go with oars than under a sail that could drive his boat hard onto a shoal. But at least the fog was thinning and the sun was visible as a great red furnace climbing into the clearer air. Maybe, I thought optimistically, a fog would shroud us when we approached our enemy and we would surprise him, and then slaughter him.

Of that, at least, I was certain. We would slaughter the enemy because we were a pair of ships loaded with battle-hardened warriors, men who had survived shield walls, men whose only trade was killing. Any settlement on the wind-swept coast would fear us. We were the wolf and the eagle come for vengeance.

Yet if the wolf and the eagle were to feed they must first find their prey, and that, I hoped, would be easy enough, because any man strong enough to send over a hundred men west to Britain would be well known among the communities that bordered the Inner Sea, but defeating that man would be a grim task.

Most of those communities lived in artificial mounds they called terpen. A terpen was a heap of wood and clay-reinforced sand that lifted its houses above the highest tides, and from their ramparts a man could see a long way. Our approaching ships would be visible, and all surprise lost, but that was a problem for another day. First we had to discover who and where our enemy was, and only then decide how to defeat him.

I was back at the steering-oar and taking *Spearhafoc* in the trail of the fishing boat, which was still an indistinct dark lump in the mist, though we could see she had entered a creek that lay between marshy banks. The men on board that boat would be able to see the wolf's head on my sail and the eagle blazoned on Egil's ship, and this coast had suffered for years from Danes scouring the sea's edge for plunder and slaves, and I did not doubt the fishermen thought we were just another such raid.

The fishing boat rounded a bend in the creek so all I could see now was her mast, but I could also see a darker patch of mist that shifted southwards with the wind. It was smoke, I realised, rising from a settlement.

'Down sail,' I called, 'and oars!'

The yard rattled down the mast, there was a brief flurry as the sail was brailed tight, then stowed along *Spearhafoc*'s midline, and then the oars were dipping and we slid into the creek that was barely wide enough, indeed so narrow that the oars were sometimes digging into the mud of the banks. *Banamaðr* followed us closely. I had given the steering-oar to Gerbruht who had been raised among these shallow creeks, and I stood beside him, peering ahead, while Egil was standing in *Banamaðr*'s prow beneath the carved eagle. Two of his Danes stood with him, both carrying the long hunting bows that could kill a stag at two or three hundred paces. They were searching the marshes on either bank, looking for an enemy who might try to dissuade us with an arrow. None came.

We turned the tight bend, though not without difficulty. I had to put six men in the prow to pole us off the bank before we found deep water again, and ahead of us was a wide, wind-shivered lake in which men were standing to cast throw nets. Or rather they had been standing, but now fled to the eastern shore where there was a palisaded settlement from which the smoke of fires smeared the sky.

'Smoking fish,' Gerbruht grunted.

'We'll buy some,' I said.

'They'll have whale meat too, lord,'

'I hate whale meat.'

'It's good, lord.'

'I'd rather eat carrots.'

He chuckled. 'Steer for the settlement?'

I nodded. The wide lake was doubtless treacherous with shallows, but withies were planted in the mud to indicate the channels, and we followed those marks to where a crude timber pier jutted from the settlement's seaward wall. A dozen fishing boats were tied to its wharf and the one we had followed was even now lashing its mooring lines and its crew of three men, having secured their ship, fled for the village.

'Look, lord,' Gerbruht said, and pointed to the shore south of the settlement, but I had already seen what had disturbed him. There were the charred bones of a dozen small fishing boats.

The gate in the palisade opened and men began emerging. About half carried shields and a few had spears. The rest had axes or reaping hooks. I counted seventy men.

'Idiots,' I said.

'Idiots?' Gerbruht sounded offended as if I had cast a slur on all Frisians.

'Easier to kill them outside the walls. Damned sight harder to kill them when they're behind the palisade.'

'We're going to fight them?'

243

'Not if I can help it.'

After three last hard strokes, our oars were shipped and Gerbruht slid *Spearhafoc* gently alongside the fishing boats. We tied the ship and watched *Banamaðr* glide in behind us.

'You stay here!' I called to my crew.

I took Gerbruht and Finan with me. We each carried a shield, but wore no mail or helmet. I had Serpent-Breath at my side, but I would leave her in her scabbard. Egil joined me with two of his men who like us carried shields, theirs painted with Egil's spread eagle. Egil's sword, Adder, was by his side, but, like his men, he was not in his battle-mail.

'I hope we don't use the swords,' I said.

'Pity,' he retorted.

'There's seventy of them, you idiot.'

'So? There's six of us.'

'And look at them,' I said, 'they're old men, not a warrior there. And they're carrying reaping hooks and fish-spears! These aren't the folk who raided the Tinan.'

'Pity.' He grinned. He was a war-Dane, never happier than when his enemy was close, but he had stayed loyal to me because I had saved his younger brother's life. Berg, that brother, was one of his two men and looked slightly nervous, though if it came to a fight he would be as vicious and relentless as Egil himself. 'And there's a bloody priest,' Egil groused.

'Of course there is,' I said, 'they're Christians. Turn your shields,' I added, and we all very ostentatiously turned our shields upside down, a signal that we came in peace.

The priest, apparently reassured by the signal, walked towards us. We had left the pier and stopped a few paces from the shore to wait for him.

'Who are you?' he asked.

'I am Egil Skallagrimmrson,' Egil chose to answer for me, then gestured at me, 'and this is my aged father, Rorik Skallagrimmrson.'

I growled and Egil grinned.

The priest looked at each of us, seeing four hammers and two crosses hanging around our necks. 'I am Father Aukil,' he said. 'Why do you come?'

'To buy ale and food,' I answered.

'We have little,' he said.

'And we have much gold,' I assured him, and opened the pouch at my sword belt to show him the coins.

'We may have some smoked fish to spare,' the priest said nervously.

'We also come,' Egil went on, 'to discover whose ships have disturbed the coast. Slaving ships.'

Father Aukil seemed to shiver and made the sign of the cross. 'Buy your food and go,' he said, and I suddenly understood the meaning of the burned ships on the shore and why there were only older men facing us.

'So the ships came here?' I asked.

'We have seal meat too,' the priest said, 'and bread.'

'Priest,' I said harshly, 'we are warriors and come with swords. Tell us about the ships that raided this settlement or we will finish the work they began.'

'Why do you want to know?' he asked.

'So we can kill them,' Egil put in wolfishly.

'You are not enough men,' the priest said. 'Others have tried, even Count Dirk sent warriors and they are all dead men now.'

I knew the count was ostensibly the ruler of Frisia, but he had small authority over the stubborn, bloody-minded communities along the coast. If I had told Æthelstan of the raid on my people he would have sent an emissary to Count Dirk, and doubtless a gift that would probably have been a goat's bone that the emissary would swear was the Virgin Mary's rib, and the count and the emissary would have talked for a month and achieved nothing. The count had evidently received a bloody nose when he had tried to exert his control and doubtless did not want another.

'How many women and children did they take?' I demanded of Father Aukil.

'Almost all, lord,' he said, evidently deciding I was of noble rank.

'You want them back?'

'They'll have gone to the slave markets already, lord. They were taken six months ago.'

'And any too sick or too weak to sell?' I demanded. 'They might yet be alive. Where do I find them?'

Father Aukil was almost in tears. 'You can't find them, lord! They find us!'

So perhaps, I thought, the priest had not lied and they really were low on food.

'They keep coming here?' I demanded. 'And take food each time?'

'Yes, lord.'

'When will they come next?'

'Any time, lord. We thought you might be them till we saw the beasts on your prows.'

'They send two ships?'

'Usually just one, lord, but sometimes two.'

And doubtless the slaver was sending ships up and down the long Inner Sea and demanding supplies from every settlement. He had no need to fish for himself, or grow crops or brew ale, he simply took what he needed and sold the surplus.

'We stay here till the ship comes,' I announced.

'No, lord!' the priest pleaded. 'If he knows his men died here . . .'

'He'll come and kill you all,' I said, 'but I'll kill him first.'

'My father, Rorik Skallagrimmrson,' Egil said, 'is a famed warrior. Men sing of him from the land of ice to the walls of Rome.'

I did not wait for the priest's agreement, but ordered Gerbruht to take six men and move *Spearhafoc* further south in the big lake and hide her in a creek among the rushes. It would mean stepping her mast and removing the carved bird from her high prow, but once in a rush-edged creek she would be invisible, as would *Banamaðr* who went with her. We took our mail, helmets and weapons off the ships first and followed a plainly unhappy Father Aukil into the settlement where racks and racks of fish were being smoked above peat fires. I gave the priest two gold coins and so bought enough ale, bread and fish to feed my men, and then we waited.

We had been given a long house as our quarters. It was stoutly built of timber with wattle and mud walls and a roof of peat sods. The floor was covered in old rushes that did not keep the damp from seeping into our sleeping bodies.

'It sometimes floods at high tides,' Father Aukil said apologetically, 'we should move the village to higher ground, but . . .' he shrugged. It seemed that since the village had been raided there was no enthusiasm or energy to make improvements.

But at least we learned something of our enemy as we waited. Father Aukil and some of the surviving villagers told us what they knew, how a man named Sikke had come to the coast with a crew of men. 'All kinds of men, lord,' Father Aukil told me, 'like yours! Frisians, Danes, Angles, Saxons, Scots, Franks, some Christian, some not!'

'Sikke,' I said, the name meant 'victory', 'is Christian?'

'He wore a cross the day I saw him, lord, but many wear the cross who deny our Saviour.'

'He calls himself the Count of the Waadsee,' one of the men told me.

'And where is he?'

It seemed Sikke had taken an old terpen and rebuilt it, strengthening the mound against the storms and tides and made a palisade around a great hall at its summit. 'Then he began his raids,' Father Aukil said helplessly. 'He takes anything he wants. Women, children, food, boats, ale, tools. Some young men have joined him. Even some of ours.'

'How many men does he have?'

'Many,' was the only answer I got, though one of the priest's companions said he had seen a dozen ships moored at Sikke's hall.

'Could be five hundred men,' Finan said.

'But not all of them warriors,' Egil said.

'You said you saw a dozen ships at Sikke's terpen,' I said to the fisherman, 'do they let your boats get near?'

He shrugged. 'If we're fishing they leave us alone, unless they want to take our catch.'

'And the slaves?' Egil asked. 'What happens to them?'

'They take them to the markets in Daneland.'

'They boasted of that when they took our young women and children,' Father Aukil said in a voice of misery.

'And Count Dirk is doing nothing more?' I asked.

They shrugged. 'We hear he has problems on his eastern frontier, lord,' the priest said, 'and one war is enough.'

So we waited.

Sikke, it seemed to me, had done what my ancestors had done, or what the Danes had done to Northumbria and East

Anglia. Adventurers had settled on the coast, made a fortress, then harried the land around until they were acknowledged as the ruler of a whole region, but Sikke had made the mistake of raiding my land. If he had stayed on the Frisian coast I would have ignored him, but doubtless because he had exhausted the settlements of the Waadsee of their children and women he was casting his net further afield.

Then, four days after we had hidden *Spearhafoc* and *Banamaðr* in a nearby creek, Sikke's men came.

They came in two small ships, each with about twenty men at the oars. It was a windless day, the Waadsee calm under a brilliant blue sky.

'A fine day for killing,' Egil murmured to me as we watched from the palisade.

Father Aukil had identified the ships as Sikke's, recognising the eagle's head crudely painted in black on their sails which, though there was no wind, hung from the yards.

'What do we do?' Finan asked me.

'What we planned,' I said.

If the approaching men followed their usual practice they would enter the village and go straight to Father Aukil's small church that lay some fifty paces from the gate and where the 'tribute' of food and ale was supposed to be waiting. I would let them go that far, then lead my men out of our long house to bar their retreat to their ships, and after that it was simply a matter of slaughter.

'Best get ready,' I said, and we went back to the long house where my servant Aldwyn brought me my best coat of Frisian mail, the links heavy, backed with leather, and edged at the neck and skirt hems with gold and silver rings. I pulled on my rich bracelets, the glittering trophies of victories past that would betray to the enemy that I was a warlord. I tugged on the heavy boots that were lined with iron strips and heeled with golden spurs. Aldwyn buckled the smaller sword belt, sewn with silver squares, that held Wasp-Sting at my right side, then the heavier belt, blazoned with gold wolf heads that held Serpent-Breath at my left hip. Around my neck I wrapped a scarf of rare white silk, a gift from Benedetta, and over it I hung a thick gold chain with an ivory hammer hanging over my heart, and next to it the gold cross that Benedetta insisted I wear because it would protect me. I fastened a night-black cloak about my shoulders, then pulled on my finest war-helm that was crested with a silver wolf. I closed the cheek-pieces so that all an enemy could see were my eyes. I was in my war-glory.

I had hesitated to bring the finery. I had plenty of older mail coats and helmets that would protect me, and dressing in my finest gear to fight mere slavers had seemed excessive, but Benedetta had insisted. 'You are a lord!' she had said. 'Let them see that! It will frighten them!' And she was surely right. To Sikke's men, accustomed to the shabby leather tunics and rusted mail coats that prevailed on the muddy margins of the Waadsee, my glittering war gear would be a nightmare. It would also be a lure. Men could become rich by killing me and stripping my corpse, but I had little fear of that on that bright morning.

I helped Aldwyn into his mail coat. He was fifteen or sixteen years old by now, old enough to fight in the shield wall. 'You stand to my right,' I told him. He looked frail, but his thin body had a sinewy strength and he was fast. Faster than me, I reckoned, but I was old and knew the years had robbed me of the quicksilver speed I had once possessed. Aldwyn pulled on one of my old helmets and I tied the cheek-pieces for him, then checked as I heard the two ships banging against the pier. 'Our guests have arrived,' I announced, 'silence!'

Egil, like me, had brought his war finery. His mail was meticulously, obsessively polished until it gleamed like silver, and his helmet was crowned with two massive eagle wings. He wore as many arm rings as I did, and his long-sword, Adder, hung at his side in a red leather scabbard.

He grinned at me. 'The bastards will shit themselves when they see us,' he remarked happily.

'And some will run,' I suggested. I reckoned that once a fight started they would flee to the flanks, scale the palisade and run to their ships, so I planned to send Egil's brother, Berg, with half a dozen men to make a shield wall across the pier. That should be enough men to seal the pier and over-come whatever ship-guards had been left behind. All Berg's men would be spear-Danes, and all of them vicious fighters.

'This is the easy day,' I told my men. 'We outnumber them and we're better warriors! They're nothing but bullies and we'll hammer them!' That was greeted with growls of approval. 'Put them down fast, but I want prisoners. Two or three will be enough. And don't be careless! They may be sheep for the slaughter, but they're still armed and desperate and I want to take you all home. So, fight as you know how to fight and enjoy yourselves!'

We watched through one of the shuttered openings in the long-house wall. The flimsy settlement gate was dragged open and I counted thirty-two men swagger through. They might swagger, but they looked ragged. At least half were in mail, though the mail was broken in places and dark with rust, the rest had leather jerkins. Most had helmets, but they were simple bowl helmets without nose- or cheek-guards. All had swords, and a dozen were carrying long heavy spears. That was weaponry enough to cow fisherfolk, but puny against my men's savagery.

I edged the long-house door open a hand's breadth and waited until the thirty-two men had made a rough line facing the church. One of them called out, demanding that the 'tribute' be brought out. That was when I walked into the open.

I went alone, carrying my wolf's head shield in my left hand and Serpent-Breath in my right. For long heartbeats none of them saw me, then one man turned and called to his companions and they all turned, astonished.

Astonished because they did not see a lone warrior facing them, instead they saw a lord of war in his battle-glory.

'You will drop your weapons and kneel down,' I shouted to them.

Instead they drew their swords, though none moved towards me, and just then Finan came from the house dressed in a black coat of mail that he had taken from a Scottish warrior at Brunanburh. He insisted that the blackened mail made him look sinister, which it did, though his most frightening aspect was the obvious joy he took in battle. He was carrying the dead Scotsman's sword that he had taken as his own and renamed Raven-Feeder. It was a much lighter blade than Serpent-Breath, but suited Finan's style of fighting, which was lethally fast, and no sooner had he taken his place to my left than Egil appeared with his spread-wing helmet and shining mail. Adder hung scabbarded at his side and in her place he carried a giant war axe with a blade polished to a dazzling shine.

Now they were faced with three lords of battle. They just stared at us in disbelief.

'Come on, boys!' Egil called to them. 'There's only three of us!'

'And if you want your tribute,' I added, 'you have to take it from us.'

Still they did not move. None carried a shield, but still they could have taken us down with the long spears holding us in place as the swordsmen surrounded us, but they were in shock.

'If this is the best Sikke has,' I said quietly, 'we'll turn him and his men into offal.'

'We will anyway,' Egil said, then turned to his right and gave a piercing whistle that brought the rest of our men out of the long house. Berg and his group of Danes ran to the pier, but the rest formed up to make a shield wall gaudy with wolf and eagle emblems. Now the frightened men were faced by a hundred warriors and whatever small bravery they had vanished like morning mist.

'Horns!' I shouted, and twenty men from either end of our wall ran forward to make new shield walls either side of the enemy huddle. Sikke's men were not quite surrounded, but they had to look left and right as well as straight ahead to see what we threatened.

'And forward!' I called, and my remaining men simply walked towards them.

They broke.

We advanced in a shield wall, our shields clattering as we paced forward. Sikke's men watched us for about four of those paces, then turned and fled. Our two horns on the enemy's flanks tried to intervene and stopped a few, but the rest vanished among the peat and reed thatched homes.

'Follow them!' I bellowed, then seized Egil's arm. 'Call Berg and his men back.'

'But . . .' he began, wanting to tell me that I had just opened a path to their ships for the fleeing enemy.

'Do it!' I snarled, unhappy to use such a tone to a friend, but Egil obeyed.

The palisade around the settlement was taller than a man and for most of its length lacked a fighting platform. It was crude and, in places, the damp had rotted the wood. It was good for keeping cattle or sheep outside, but as a defence against warriors it was pathetic. Or, for that matter, for keeping warriors inside the village, which was where Sikke's men were trapped. They fled to the palisade and used their weapons to pry the stakes apart or to hack gaps where the rotted wood was darkest.

'You're letting them escape?' Egil asked as we ran between the houses. He had sent a messenger to his brother and had caught up with me.

'A few,' I said.

'Why?'

'So we can kill them all,' I said savagely.

Ahead of me now was a knot of men crowding to a place where a gap had been torn in the palisade. Some had already escaped, the rest were jostling and pushing to reach the gap and then they saw us coming. A young man screamed a warning, then bravely charged me with a spear. I turned my shield just as he lunged and his spear was deflected to my left side and I let him run onto Serpent-Breath's blade which pierced his belly to jar against his spine. I kicked his body off the blade and followed Egil who was carving a bloody path into the fugitives with his huge axe. Finan was beside him, his Raven-Feeder moving lightning fast. Another dozen of my men were swiftly turning the panicked crowd into a pile of corpses.

254

'Go,' I told Aldwyn. Some battle practice, even against an already defeated enemy, would do him good, and I went with him, fended off a feeble sword lunge from an older man, then hit him hard with my shield boss, rammed Serpent-Breath into the earth and reached out to seize the man by the collar of his leather jerkin. I dragged him back from the maul, kicked his legs out from beneath him, then retrieved Serpent-Breath. 'Aldwyn!' I called, then pulled him back from a corpse he was hacking with his spear-blade. 'That bugger's dead, but keep this one alive.' I pointed to the older man. 'I want him alive!'

'Yes, lord.'

I kicked the older man's sword out of his hand, reckoned that none of my men needed any help, and walked to the settlement's gate where a frightened Father Aukil was peering at the wharf through a small gap between the gates. Not that he needed the gap, the two gates were so decayed and ramshackle that there were gaps between every timber.

'Some of them are escaping, lord!' the priest said, excited.

'Good.'

'Good?' He sounded shocked.

'Excellent,' I said. I dragged one of the flimsy gates fully open and watched men scrambling down the pier and leaping into one of the boats that had brought them. Thirty-two men had come to the village and twelve were leaving. I watched as the twelve rowed their small ship into the north breeze and against the current. 'They'll have a long hard row,' I said, amused.

Egil had joined me. 'Want me to pursue them in *Banamaðr*?' he asked.

'No. I want them to get safe home.'

He spat. 'This was too easy.'

'Nonsense,' I teased him, 'you can write a song about your great victory over the Lord of the Waadsee!'

'Ha!' He sneered, then scooped up a handful of grass to clean the blade of Adder that was blood-smeared to the hilt.

'And the first line of your song,' I went on, 'should say how Uhtred, Lord of the Northern Seas, led his fierce men across the water.'

'You think I'll even mention you? Look at the bastards! Getting clean away.'

'And they'll be back,' I said softly, 'to write the last verse of your song.'

He understood then and laughed. 'You want them to come to us!'

'Of course. It will take us two or three days to find Sikke's terpen, and once we've found it we have to decide how to assault it. He'll have seen us coming, he almost certainly outnumbers us, and I don't want a song written about how Uhtred of Bebbanburg died attacking a strongly held fortress in the Inner Sea. I want a song of slaughter.'

Egil looked at the feeble palisade. 'You think we can defend this place?'

'I think we have to. The song depends on it.'

The song of slaughter.

It was simple really. Our enemy, Sikke, had upwards of three hundred and fifty men left, at least according to our three prisoners who talked volubly when Egil offered to loosen their tongues with a branding iron he had heated to a red glow. Of those three hundred and fifty only around half were trained warriors, the rest manned the oars or carried spears to support the warriors in the front rank.

'It's simple,' I had told my men when the brawl in the village was over, 'we have a hundred men and we can either assault Sikke's fortress and fight men who have a stout palisade to protect them, or we can defend this place and make them do the attacking.'

'A child of seven could knock this palisade down,' one of Egil's men said scornfully. 'It doesn't even have a fighting platform!'

'And the front gate,' Finan added, 'couldn't keep a crippled sheep out!'

'Today is Tiwesdæg,' I said. 'The men who escaped will get back by this evening, and Sikke, if he has any brain at all, will send men south on Wodnesdæg to look at this place. We let them look. They will go back late Wodnesdæg and Sikke will make his plans on Thunresdæg and probably Frigedæg too. So the earliest I expect them is dawn on Sæternesdæg. The earliest! He could well come later, but I imagine he'll want to bring his boats down at night to surprise us at first light. Father Aukil,' I turned to the priest, 'this afternoon I daresay there'll be nobody watching us, so I want you to get a dozen fishermen and have them move the channel markers.'

'The withies?' the priest asked.

'Move them so they lead into shallow water. Twicca,' I turned to the fisherman, 'you know what I want?'

'I do, lord.'

'Help them. I want to strand Sikke's ships.'

'Pleasure, lord.' Twicca had been cheered by the news that the captives taken from the Tinan were still at Sikke's hall, held there until more captives could be taken to assemble a large enough number to carry to the slave market. Conversely Twicca was dispirited that I was not planning an immediate raid on Sikke's terpen, but the thought of clambering up a

terpen's steep side to assail a defended rampart had no appeal
to me. I needed to draw Sikke out and fight on ground of my
own choosing.

Which gave me four or five days to prepare that ground,
for which we needed timber and muscle. I pulled down two
of the abandoned houses and used their timbers to strengthen
the walls and make fighting platforms either side of the gate.
We deliberately left the half rotted timbers of the gate as they
were, and similarly did not repair the ramshackle palisade on
either side of the gate, instead making a new palisade hard up
against the old so that Sikke, when he came, would see the
decayed entrance flanked by rotten fencing. 'You think he'll
attack there?' Finan asked me.

'I think he'll take the easy choice,' I said. I had placed
barrels around the palisade so that men could stand on them
and so appear to be on a fighting platform. To an attacker,
coming from the wide sea-lake, it would seem that the least
garrisoned part of the village's wall was the main gate. To
me that would have spelled trouble, but I somehow doubted
that Sikke would recognise the trap. He was a bully who
despised the communities he claimed as his own, and his first
ambition would be to overwhelm Father Aukil's village and
then punish it. True he knew that somehow Father Aukil
had recruited close to a hundred hardened warriors, but he
outnumbered us and doubtless believed he would leave the
devastated village with new slaves and a heap of expensive
war gear.

Just inside the main gate we dug a pit the same width as
the gate and almost as deep as a sword-blade, though the pit
flooded before we could finish the excavation. We put sharpened stakes into the base, then covered the pit with thin
withies, which, in turn, were covered by rushes over which

we scattered sand. To our eyes the pit looked obvious, but to battle-fevered men, bursting through the gate, it would probably be invisible.

'Will it work?' Finan asked sceptically.

'By the time Sikke gets through the gate,' I said, 'he'll be mad with anger and want nothing but revenge.'

'I hope you're right.'

'So do I.'

We put two planks over the pit so the fishermen could go to their boats without using the back gate, and on the Thunresdæg we saw a strange ship in the channel that lay beyond the lake's further side. I suspected it was a fishing craft come to spy on us and I made sure that men used the planks to walk in and out of the gate. If Sikke had any sense he would scout the village and I suspected the crew of the fishing boat had landed on the seaward island and were watching us from among the reeds. None of us wore mail or helmets, and Egil had the mischievous idea of dressing some of his smaller men in women's clothing so that the watchers would believe there were women they had missed in their first raid.

The fishing boat stayed all day, only going northwards as dusk was falling.

'So he's seen us,' I said. 'Tomorrow he makes his plans and tomorrow night he sails.'

'He won't come into the channel till daylight,' Twicca said, 'he can't see the channel at night.'

I nodded. 'So dawn on Sæternesdæg.'

'Or dusk tomorrow,' Egil put in.

'One or the other,' I said, 'but one thing is certain. He'll come.'

*   *   *

Sikke did not come. A whole week passed and I was tired of eating salt fish and hard bread. The village's ale was thin and sour, like my mood. I had been so certain of the enemy's response and had been proved entirely wrong.

'Perhaps the bugger isn't there?' Finan said. 'Perhaps he's gone north to sell his slaves?'

'Either that or he's raising men,' Egil suggested.

Egil's suggestion was the least welcome, because if the survivors of the brief fight in the village had persuaded him that we were a truly formidable enemy then he could well be paying Danish warriors to fight for him.

'And if he's not at home,' Egil went on, 'why don't we pay his home a visit?'

That tempted me. If we took *Spearhafoc* and *Banamaðr* north we might well find Sikke's terpen inadequately guarded and a fast assault might overwhelm his men and give us whatever riches were inside. It was very tempting, but my instinct rejected the idea.

'He's coming,' I insisted.

I worried that my caution was because of age. In truth I was not entirely sure how old I was, except that I was too old. My grandfather, Uhtred the Wise, had lived to be eighty-six, an extraordinary age, and I suspected I was close to that, and knew I was not the warrior I had been. At night, half sleeping in the long house, I would remember past battles. It did not matter that those battles had been mostly victories, my mind insisted on the moments when I had almost died. When a shield had been slammed aside and a spear-blade lanced at my belly, or when a long-handled axe had cut from above, and I would shudder at those memories and wonder if they were omens being sent by the gods. I thought of Benedetta, doubtless wondering what was happening, and imagined a survivor of my men finally reaching Bebbanburg to tell her that my body was in a shallow Frisian grave, and I would reach out and grasp Serpent-Breath's hilt as if to assure myself that when that end came I would be transported to Valhalla. Yet next morning, when men grumbled at the waiting, I would still insist, 'He's coming.' And in my head I would think, 'He's coming and he will kill me.'

Then he came.

Fog had rolled in from the sea, a thick dark fog that chilled us. I was pulling on my armour, assisted by Aldwyn, not because I expected Sikke's arrival, but because it was a precaution we took every day, when Finan came though the long-house door. 'They're here,' he said happily, 'six ships.'

'How big?'

'Small, thirty or forty men in each.'

So between a hundred and eighty and two hundred and forty men.

Egil came through the door a moment later. 'They're aground!' he said wolfishly. 'Or at least three of them are.'

Berg, Egil's brother, was next. 'They're wading ashore, lord,' he announced.

'Good,' I muttered. Men soaked to the waist were sluggish and poor fighters. 'What are they?' I asked Egil as Aldwyn brought my heavy boots.

'Same as before,' he said, 'about half have mail and look capable, the rest are ragged-arsed spearmen without shields.'

Untrained men were usually issued spears, and Egil meant that their dress was ragged and their only protection was, at best, leather. Such men would prove easy enough to kill, but in numbers and protected by trained warriors they could be lethal.

I stamped my boots and buckled Serpent-Breath at my waist, Aldwyn stood on a stool to lower my helmet over my head, then I picked up my shield. 'We'd best be out there,' I said.

At that moment the enemy could not see any of us. Our sentries had spotted their ships, then dropped down from the new fighting platforms beside the flimsy gate and now we watched them from between the trunks of the palisade. Sikke must have thought we were still sleeping. Four of his ships were stranded on the falling tide, but two others had found the real channel and were rowing for the pier. They crunched into the moored fishing boats and men leaped onto the wharf and began running down the pier to join the half-soaked men who had waded ashore.

'That must be Sikke,' Finan muttered beside me.

'The tall fellow?'

'In the white cloak.'

It seemed likely to me. The tall fellow was indeed tall and dressed in a long mail coat over which he wore a white cloak. His helmet glittered in the foggy air and was surmounted by a crest of black feathers. His shield was white with an eagle's head painted in black. His sword was drawn. For the moment he seemed content to wait as his men assembled, and I turned and nodded to Gerbruht. 'Now!'

We had assembled two dozen goats in the narrow space between the hidden pit and the gates, and Gerbruht, dressed in only a fisherman's smock, now pushed open one of the gates and herded the goats out of the settlement. To the watching enemy it must have seemed as though another day was just starting at the village as livestock, brought behind the palisade for protection overnight, was let out for a day's foraging. Gerbruht followed them, leaving the gate open, then pretended to see the enemy not a hundred paces away. He gawped at them for a moment, then fled back into the village and hurried off to the long house to don his armour. He left the gates open.

'Now come, you bastard,' I muttered. I wanted Sikke to see the obvious invitation to assault the open gate where all my men were gathered, which meant the sides and rear of the village were unprotected. My own men were in two shield walls either side of the pit, hidden by the palisade, but ready to close up behind the pit and strip away the two planks. Egil's men were crouched low on the fighting platforms that we had repaired. There they had all our spears and Egil's two huntsmen with their vicious longbows had joined them.

I now joined my own men in one of the shield walls, standing in the front rank with young Aldwyn to my right and Finan to my left. 'Think they'll be stupid enough?' Finan muttered.

'Yes,' I said, and hoped I was right.

Egil was still peering through the palisade to the right of the gate. He looked at me, held up two fingers and then used them to make a walking gesture, which I took to mean that two men were approaching.

I drew Serpent-Breath and wondered if this was her last fight. I kissed the blade where the strange patterns had suggested her name, then rested her tip on the pit's edge. If I had understood Egil's gestures then Sikke had taken the precaution of sending two scouts to probe the gate, and at that moment the rushes and sand covering the pit looked monstrously false to me and I feared the scouts would see through the deception. I raised two fingers to Egil, who was alternately glancing at me and at the approaching men, then drew Serpent-Breath across my throat.

Egil grinned, and, in answer, blew me a kiss that made my men laugh.

Egil had been crouched on the fighting platform, but now jumped down. He held a finger to his mouth, indicating we should be silent, then leaped across the corner of the pit so he was standing in the open gateway. He, like me, was in his war-glory, in his shining mail and with his helmet crowned by the eagle's wings. He carried no shield, but Adder, his sword, was in his right hand.

Egil was enjoying himself. He was a born warrior and a lethal one, and he loved nothing more than an audience. He loved to entertain us in the feast hall, playing a harp as he chanted his own songs about fields turned red with battle, and now he was alone in the village's entrance with my men watching and, in a moment, all Sikke's men watching too.

'By the time it's a song,' Finan said in a low voice, 'it won't be two men coming, but twenty.'

'No,' I said reprovingly, 'a hundred at least.'

Gerbruht pushed through my two ranks to take his place the other side of Aldwyn. He was in his mail, helmeted, and carrying a massive war axe. 'What's happening?' he asked.

'Jarl Egil,' Finan said, 'is about to win the battle for us.'

Egil strolled into the centre of the wide-open gateway and stood there, letting Adder's sharp tip rest on the ground as he stared at the two approaching men. The two just gawped at Egil in his glittering war-glory. Then both men retreated. They did not go far, just a few paces, but their fear was obvious. They had doubtless heard of the warriors who had killed their companions a couple of weeks earlier, but seeing one facing

264

them was still a shock. They were warriors themselves, or at least they were in mail, had swords scabbarded at their sides and had good helmets.

Egil laughed at them. 'You want to come in?' he called. 'You're welcome!' He pushed one of the gates further open and gestured into the village. 'Come! You're welcome!'

I had gone to the gate's edge and was peering through the crack between the gate and its post. I could see Sikke, who was just staring at his two men and the single warrior who opposed them. He must have feared that the one man was not alone, that more warriors waited for him, and that meant the nightmare of a shield-wall battle and I doubted that Sikke, self-proclaimed Count of the Waadsee, had faced many shield walls. His prey was defenceless villagers, but he had evidently defeated a force sent by the Count of Frisia so he was not entirely ignorant of the danger.

Meanwhile Egil was taunting the two men. 'I don't blame you for running away,' he explained in a reasonable voice, 'I know you're fearsome when you fight against women and children, but fighting against a spear-Dane? That's beyond your skills. You're probably pissing yourselves with terror now, and that's understandable too, but if you drop your swords and kneel down then the terror will be over. Or you can just run away? Run back to that turd Sikke and tell him you were frightened by one man.'

The taunts worked because both men ran at Egil. I smiled. I did not care how good the two were, they would be no match for the Dane who stood waiting for them. The two were angry and they were impetuous. And doomed.

Egil stepped to his left an instant before they reached him. He parried the wild hack the closest man gave him, then killed him with a backswing of Adder into the nape of the neck. It

265

was so fast that I could scarce follow. Egil was as quick as Finan in a fight, and that speed made him deadly.

'Nice,' Finan muttered beside me.

The second man tried a backswing of his own, a scything cut aimed at Egil's stomach, but Egil just stepped away from it, then immediately stepped forward again and Adder lanced out in a swift lunge that pierced mail, leather, muscle and belly. That was followed by a mighty kick into the man's groin that helped Egil drag Adder out of the wound. The man's sword hand faltered, his weapon dropped and Egil finished him with a contemptuous slash to the throat. Then he picked up both fallen swords and tossed them back over the pit before turning and facing Sikke. He held his arms wide, as if signalling that the death of the two men had been easy, and then he bowed, just as he did when acknowledging a feast hall of warriors responding to one of his songs. It was that elegant and insolent gesture that spurred Sikke to the attack. I heard him roar, saw him flourish his sword, then charge.

They all came, and Egil did not move.

He stayed bowed down, apparently staring at the ground, as Sikke and his men pounded closer. There were roughly two hundred of them, just over twice our number, but more than half of Sikke's men were not in mail and only about a quarter had shields and helmets. They were howling as they ran and they were doing it all wrong. 'Like facing Scottish bastards,' Finan said drily.

'Thank God they're not Scots,' I said.

'They'd be worse,' Finan agreed.

The Scots tended to favour a wild, howling charge that was terrifying, but left them ragged when they struck a shield wall. The sheer fury of their charge could split a shield wall, but because they did not all arrive simultaneously it was easy enough for the second rank to despatch the men who had done the damage and seal up the front rank. Sikke's men, on the other hand, were not charging with the passion and hatred that animated the Scots, but rather, I suspected, out of a misplaced belief that it was their best tactic.

I had encouraged that belief by concealing my men either side of the gate where the palisade hid them, which meant Sikke and his men could only see Egil, who still, apparently, just stared at the ground.

'Move, you idiot!' Finan muttered, looking at Egil, who still ignored the approaching enemy, but then Egil suddenly straightened, ran three paces to his right and leaped up to the fighting platform. He made that leap in his mail and it was a remarkable feat, and as he reached the fighting platform he seized a spear and hurled it at Sikke. Sikke managed to catch the spear-blade on his shield, but the sheer force of the blow almost threw him backwards. He stumbled as his men raced past him, still howling defiance.

'Shields!' I called, and we all picked up our heavy shields and overlapped them with a clatter. 'And move!'

My two groups of men closed from either side to make a shield wall two or three paces behind the pit. The wall was only two ranks with twenty-two men in each, but every man was in mail, helmeted, and armed with sword, axe or spear.

Sikke's leading men slowed when they saw the shield wall form, but the men behind screamed them on and Sikke himself had recovered from Egil's spear-throw and bellowed for our deaths. He could see how few we were and had no idea that as many enemies were hidden on the fighting platforms. His men crowded through the gate, still coming recklessly, and the pit opened up beneath them.

The howls turned to screams or bellows of alarm. Some

men were impaled on the stakes, others found themselves deep in the muddy trap, yet still they tried to reach us, but now they had to fight upwards from the pit and my shield wall advanced to its edge and the killing began. Their swords or axes beat harmlessly against our shields as we stabbed downwards, turning the churned pit red. More men were forced into the pit's wreckage as they were pressed from behind. It was chaos, and Egil watched it from above, judging his moment.

Sikke had somehow avoided the pit, but he recognised disaster when he saw it. He began shouting and gesticulating.

'He's taking his men around the palisade,' Finan said.

'He's trying to,' I agreed.

'Now!' Egil bellowed, and his men began jumping from the fighting platform, but going outside the palisade. Twenty-five men went out on the right and the same number on the left, and those two groups now attacked inwards.

Sikke's men were crowded just outside the gate, most of them uncertain of what was happening. The best of his warriors, the men with helmets, mail and shields, had led the charge and too many of those were now in the pit or stuck at its further side, which meant that the least experienced of the enemy were at the rear and they were now attacked by two groups of well-trained Danish warriors.

'Back!' I called to my men. 'Hold the shield wall! Back!'

'What?' Finan said as he backed away from the pit beside me.

'We can't cross the pit and keep the wall tight,' I said, 'so they can come to us.'

We went back twenty paces. There was chaos outside the gate. Egil's men were hacking their way into the panicked crowd and Sikke had lost all control of the fight, but then saw the space we offered him. He began shouting at his nearest men, his best men, and one by one they either ventured into the pit or leaped across its nearest corner. Those who crossed the pit did it by stepping on the bodies of the dead or wounded, but they made the nearer side safely, where they gathered around Sikke who stood tall in his mail. Some forty men joined him. Those men just gazed at us. They had escaped Egil's slaughter, but now faced an unbroken shield wall. If Sikke had possessed a glimmer of sense he would have led them around the flank of that shield wall, but his pride and his belligerence drove him to defiance. If he could defeat my men he would gain rich plunder in mail, helmets and weapons, let alone the arm rings and other treasures my men wore such as buckles, brooches and silver scabbards. I pushed Serpent-Breath into her richly encrusted scabbard and drew Wasp-Sting. The shorter blade was much more effective in a fight between shield walls.

'Now forward,' I said, 'shields tight!'

'Shield wall!' Sikke shouted and his men shuffled into a line and clashed their shields together.

'The last shield wall,' I said to Finan.

'Not much of one.'

'Probably the best old men can hope for,' I said. 'Take them forward.'

'Step!' Finan shouted. 'Step! Step! Step!' Each word dictating a single step, and, as we neared Sikke's wall, he said the word faster so we would hasten over the last few paces, 'Step! Step! And kill!'

Sikke had advanced just two paces to meet us, and that saved his men from being shoved back into the pit when the shield walls clashed. There was a bellow of sound as iron-bossed willow shields slammed together and as Sikke's men were shoved back a pace, then swords, seaxes and spears slid between shields to find an enemy. Axes glittered overhead either trying to split a helmet or snag a shield and drag it down. An axe blade caught Aldwyn's shield.

'Let it go down, lad,' I told him and he allowed the enemy to pull the shield down and I took a half-step to my right and slid Wasp-Sting into the man's ribs. 'Up again,' I said to Aldwyn, 'and finish the bugger off.'

The man had fallen to his knees and Aldwyn rammed his half-spear's blade into his throat.

'Well done,' I said, 'but keep your shield touching mine.'

'Push!' Sikke was bellowing at his men, hoping to shove us backwards, but we were two ranks against his one and they had neither the strength nor the skill to defeat us. Besides, half their attention was behind them where Egil's men had destroyed the remaining enemy and were now crossing the pit to join the fight.

I was facing a red-bearded warrior who spat insults at me through his four remaining teeth. He kept hammering my shield with a long-sword, lunging it again and again as if hoping to batter a hole through the willow, and I was content to let him keep doing it until he made a last mistake, but suddenly a hand reached out from the enemy's wall and grabbed the silver wolf that crowned my helmet. The man pulled, plainly hoping he could drag the helmet clear of my head, and I was jerked sideways so that the red-bearded man's next lunge slid off the edge of my shield and tore a hole in the mail at my waist. The man drew the sword back ready to give a killing lunge, but Aldwyn covered the gap with his shield just as I flicked Wasp-Sting up and slashed it across my face so that her wickedly sharp blade severed the hand of the man gripping my helmet. There was a spurt of bright blood, a scream, and I was unhampered and, tired of the red-bearded man's insults, I lowered my shield and rammed it towards his legs. He instinctively lowered his own shield and Wasp-Sting's reddened blade lunged over both shields to pierce the man's mail and I twisted the blade as it sought his heart. And found it.

I realised I was bellowing insults as I fought and was enjoying myself. I had feared age would slow me, but in truth age had equipped me. I had faced the most savage shield walls that northern warriors could bring against me. I had fought Danes, Saxons, Norsemen, Welshmen and Scots, and those years of fighting had given me weapon-skill. Even before I dropped my shield to lure the red-bearded man I was judging the man behind him, planning his death. I might not be as fast as I once was, and I knew my muscles would ache for days, but I was still Uhtredærwe, Uhtred the Wicked, and as the next man stumbled on the red-bearded warrior's corpse I flicked Wasp-Sting up and sliced his throat. 'Come!' I shouted at another enemy and saw him hesitate.

A youngster in a leather-padded jerkin was assaulting Aldwyn's shield with an axe, chopping great lumps from the boards, and I moved my own shield to cover Aldwyn's when suddenly the axe-wielding youngster gave a strangled cry and fell to his knees. A spear-blade had appeared in his chest, thrust clean through from the back and I saw one of Egil's Danes grinning happily.

And the fight was over, all but for a bloody few moments as Egil's men despatched the wounded.

'Not much of a fight,' Egil groused to me.

'It will be a great victory when you turn it into a song,' I suggested.

271

'It will be bigger than Brunanburh!' he agreed happily. 'How we crossed the whale's path to soak the Frisian coast in blood. I might even mention you.'

'You bloody well better,' I said.

Next day we took *Spearhafoc* and *Banamaðr* north through the Waadsee to find Sikke's hall. Sikke was dead, his belly ripped open by Finan's quick sword. He had only left a score of men to guard his terpen and they meekly surrendered the place without a fight. We found more than a hundred slaves imprisoned in reed-thatched huts, including all those who had been taken from my land. Twicca was reunited with his Ella and with his children, watched by a resentful Gerbruht.

'She's not really fat,' I said to Finan as I watched Twicca and his wife.

'The lass isn't small,' he said scornfully.

'No, but I've seen fatter.'

'She's probably lost weight,' Finan remarked, 'can't think Sikke fed her well.'

'Probably nothing but vegetables,' I agreed.

'Poor woman,' Finan said. 'Home, then?'

Home with Sikke's treasure, which was more than worth the voyage. I shared that trove with all the men who had crossed the sea with me. We sailed back happy, *Spearhafoc* riding a warm southern wind that sped us to Bebbanburg under a clear sky and I looked up at the stars and thought I had fought my last fight, faced my last shield wall, and was racing home to a loving woman, to good ale, and to Bebbanburg.

Wyrd bið ful ãræd

Fate is inexorable

Also by Bernard Cornwell

The LAST KINGDOM Series
(formerly The WARRIOR Chronicles)
The Last Kingdom
The Pale Horseman
The Lords of the North
Sword Song
The Burning Land
Death of Kings
The Pagan Lord
The Empty Throne
Warriors of the Storm
The Flame Bearer
War of the Wolf
Sword of Kings
War Lord

Azincourt

The GRAIL QUEST Series
Harlequin
Vagabond
Heretic

1356

Stonehenge

The Fort

The STARBUCK Chronicles
Rebel
Copperhead
Battle Flag
The Bloody Ground

The WARLORD Chronicles
The Winter King
Enemy of God
Excalibur

Fools and Mortals

Gallows Thief

A Crowning Mercy
Fallen Angels
(Originally published under the name Susannah Kells, the
pseudonym of Bernard Cornwell and his wife, Judy.)

Non-fiction
Waterloo: The History of Four Days,
Three Armies and Three Battles